Student Interactive

W9-BPQ-958

myView
LITERACY
3

SAVVAS
LEARNING COMPANY

ISBN-13: 978-0-134-90882-3
ISBN-10: 0-134-90882-1

8   21

Julie Coiro, Ph.D.

Jim Cummins, Ph.D.

Pat Cunningham, Ph.D.

Elfrieda Hiebert, Ph.D.

Pamela Mason, Ed.D.

Ernest Morrell, Ph.D.

P. David Pearson, Ph.D.

Frank Serafini, Ph.D.

Alfred Tatum, Ph.D.

Sharon Vaughn, Ph.D.

Judy Wallis, Ed.D.

Lee Wright, Ed.D.

Environments

Interactions

Environments

Essential Question

How does our
environment affect us?

▶ **Watch**

"Where We Live, Who We Are"

TURN and **TALK**
How would you describe
your environment?

SAVVAS
realize™
Go ONLINE for
all lessons.

- ▶ VIDEO
- 🔊 AUDIO
- 👆 INTERACTIVITY
- 🎮 GAME
- ✏️ ANNOTATE
- 📖 BOOK
- 🔍 RESEARCH

Spotlight on Traditional Tales

READING WORKSHOP

READING-WRITING BRIDGE

- Academic Vocabulary • Word Study
- **Read Like a Writer** • **Write for a Reader**
- Spelling • Language and Conventions

WRITING WORKSHOP

- Introduce and Immerse • Develop Elements   **Personal Narrative**
- Develop Structure • Writer's Craft
- Publish, Celebrate, and Assess

PROJECT-BASED INQUIRY

- Inquire • Research • Collaborate

Independent Reading

Reading is a skill that gets better with practice. In this unit, you will read with your teacher. You will also choose texts to read independently.

Follow these steps to help you choose a text you will enjoy reading on your own.

Step 1 Establish a purpose for reading by asking yourself the following questions. Then, set your purpose by writing it in your notebook.

- Do I want to read to learn about something?
- Do I want to read just to have fun?
- Do I want to read more books by my favorite author?

Step 2 Choose a text that fits your purpose. Be sure to select a text you will be able to read. One way to choose a text is to practice a strategy called I PICK. If most of your answers are yes, you are ready to read. Use the I PICK strategy when it is time to choose a text.

I	I choose a book.
P	**Purpose:** Why do I want to read this book?
I	**Interest:** Am I interested in this book?
C	**Comprehension:** Do I understand what I am reading?
K	**Know:** Do I know most of the words?

Independent Reading Log

Date	Book	Genre	Pages Read	Minutes Read	My Ratings
					☆☆☆☆☆

Unit Goals

Shade in the circle to rate how well you meet each goal now.

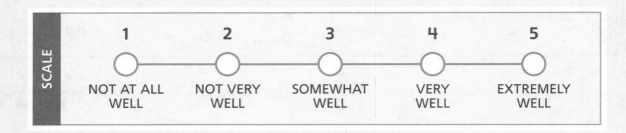

SCALE	1	2	3	4	5
	○	○	○	○	○
	NOT AT ALL WELL	NOT VERY WELL	SOMEWHAT WELL	VERY WELL	EXTREMELY WELL

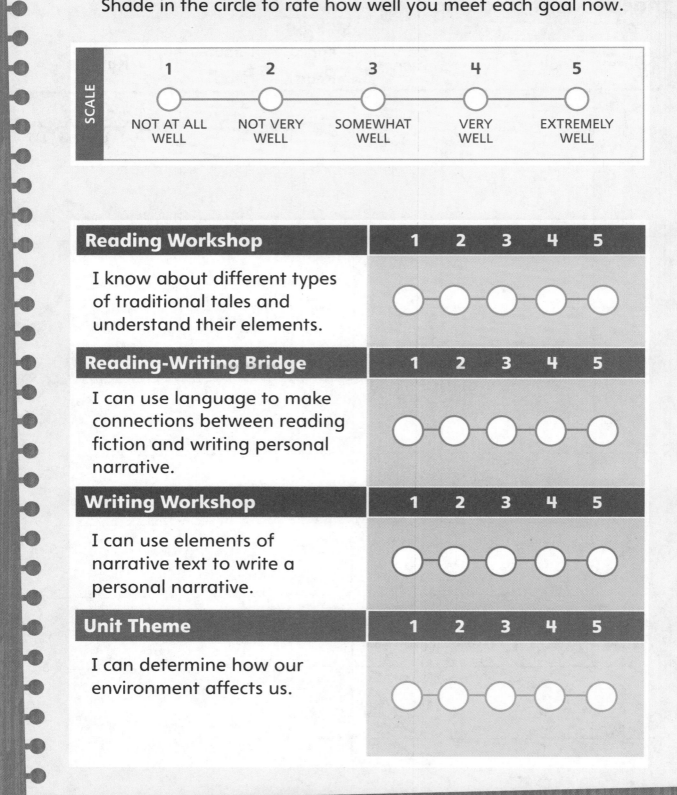

Reading Workshop	1	2	3	4	5
I know about different types of traditional tales and understand their elements.	○	○	○	○	○

Reading-Writing Bridge	1	2	3	4	5
I can use language to make connections between reading fiction and writing personal narrative.	○	○	○	○	○

Writing Workshop	1	2	3	4	5
I can use elements of narrative text to write a personal narrative.	○	○	○	○	○

Unit Theme	1	2	3	4	5
I can determine how our environment affects us.	○	○	○	○	○

Academic Vocabulary

Use these vocabulary words to talk and write about this unit's theme, *Environments: competition, solve, custom, occasion,* and *organization.*

TURNandTALK Read the words and definitions. Then make a connection between each set of words shown. What other connections can you make between the words?

competition—the act of trying to win something

solve—to find the answer to a problem

custom—something that people have done for a long time

occasion—a special time or event

organization—the process of putting things in order

Competition and **organization** are connected because

_____

_____.

Custom and **occasion** are connected because

_____

_____

_____.

Occasion and **organization** are connected because

_____

_____.

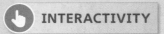
INTERACTIVITY

Going from HERE TO THERE

INDIA'S ENVIRONMENT The environment refers to the natural surroundings of a place. An environment may include landforms, weather, soil, and plant or animal life.

India is a country in Asia. The people of India get from place to place in many ways.

Ganges River

North Indian Plain

The **North Indian Plain** is a flat land where many people live. In the cities, people can travel by car or train.

Thar Desert

INDIA

The **Thar Desert** lies in the west part of India. People travel across the dry, sandy desert on camels.

Dense forest

India has **forests**, including tropical rainforests. People can move with their herds on trails and roads, mostly on foot.

14

The **Himalayas** form the tallest mountains in the world. People travel short distances on foot. They use horses or pack mules to carry supplies.

Himalayas

Ganges River

Many other rivers join the **Ganges** River, pouring in melted snow from the Himalayas. Some rivers can be crossed in boats.

Weekly Question

How do people travel in different environments?

Turn and Talk Compare the environments where you live to those shown on the map. What are some ways you go from one place to another? Make connections to your personal experiences. Discuss your ideas with a partner, following language conventions to communicate ideas effectively. This includes speaking with proper grammar, correct sentence structure, and logical word order.

Learning Goal

I can learn more about traditional tales and analyze plot and setting in a traditional tale.

Traditional Tales

Learn to recognize the literary elements of traditional tales. A **traditional tale** is a made-up story that has been told and retold many times. It includes

- A familiar **setting,** or the time and place of the story
- **Characters,** or the people or animals in a story
- A **conflict,** or problem, between people or animals
- A **plot,** or series of events, that often explains something or teaches a lesson

Look for animal characters that speak and act like real people!

TURN and **TALK**   Describe your favorite traditional tale to a partner. Use the Traditional Tales Anchor Chart to help you explain your tale. Take notes on your discussion.

 **My NOTES** _____

_____

_____

_____

_____

_____

Traditional Tales Anchor chart

* **Purpose** → To entertain, explain, or teach a lesson

* **Types of Traditional Tales**

  ○ **FOLKTALES** are another name for traditional tales that include stories shared among people that tell about their culture.

  ○ **FABLES** are stories that teach a lesson.

  ○ **FAIRY TALES** are stories with enchanted, make-believe characters and events.

  ○ **LEGENDS** are stories about the great deeds of heroes.

  ○ **MYTHS** are stories that explain something about nature.

Chitra Banerjee Divakaruni is an award-winning author and poet who was born in Kolkata, India. She now lives in Houston, Texas, and teaches creative writing. Her children's book *Grandma and the Great Gourd* was inspired by and is dedicated to her beloved dog, Juno!

Grandma and the Great Gourd

Preview Vocabulary

As you read *Grandma and the Great Gourd*, pay attention to these vocabulary words. Notice how they provide clues to the action and setting.

fierce	**baring**
flexing	**crouching**	**swipe**

Read

Before you begin reading a **traditional tale**, establish a purpose for reading the text. Follow these strategies when you read a text the first time.

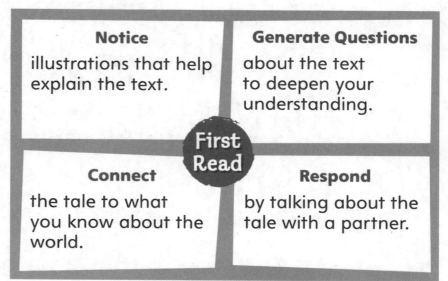

Notice illustrations that help explain the text.

Generate Questions about the text to deepen your understanding.

First Read

Connect the tale to what you know about the world.

Respond by talking about the tale with a partner.

GRANDMA
AND THE GREAT GOURD

retold by CHITRA BANERJEE DIVAKARUNI
illustrated by SUSY PILGRIM WATERS

A Bengali Folktale

AUDIO

ANNOTATE

19

1   Once upon a time, in a little village in India, there lived an old woman whom everyone called Grandma. She loved gardening and had the best vegetable patch in the village.

2   Grandma lived by herself in a little hut at the edge of the village, next to a deep, dark jungle. At times she could hear herds of elephants lumbering on forest paths, *thup-thup-thup*, or giant lizards slithering over dry leaves, *khash-khash*.

3   She didn't mind because she had two loyal dogs, Kalu and Bhulu, to protect her. They also helped her with garden chores.

Analyze Plot and Setting

Underline details that help you picture where the story takes place. Based on these details, what is the story's setting? Briefly explain the influence of the setting on the plot.

Analyze Plot and Setting

<u>Underline</u> details that help you understand that Grandma's daughter lives in a different place.

fierce wild or dangerous

4   One day, Grandma received a letter from her daughter, who lived on the other side of the jungle.

5   "Please come and visit me," said the letter. "I haven't seen you in so long. I miss you."

6   Grandma missed her daughter, too, and decided to visit her. She was a little scared about traveling through the jungle where so many fierce animals lived. But then she said, "What's life without a little adventure?"

7   She packed her things and said good-bye to her dogs. "Don't worry, boys," she told them, "I'll be back soon! Don't forget to take care of my garden." "*Gheu-gheu*!" said the dogs. "We won't forget! We'll chase away all the wild animals, and we'll listen for you. If you get in trouble, just call for us."

Use Text Evidence

Highlight a detail that suggests that Grandma's dogs plan to protect her from possible danger.

Analyze Plot and Setting

Underline details in the text that suggest that Grandma might be in danger.

baring showing

Use Text Evidence

Highlight details that describe how Grandma stops the fox from eating her.

8   As Grandma was traveling through the jungle, *khut-khut-khut*, she came upon a clever red fox.

9   "Ah, Grandma!" he said, baring his pointy teeth and smacking his lips. "How nice of you to arrive just when I'm so hungry!"

10   Grandma's heart went *dhip-dhip*, but she didn't let the fox see how scared she was.

11   "If you're planning to have me for breakfast," she said, "that's a terrible idea. See how skinny I am? I'll be a lot plumper on my way back from my daughter's house because she's such a good cook. You can eat me then, if you like."

12   "That sounds good!" said the fox, and he let her go.

13 Grandma walked deeper into the jungle, *khut-khut-khut*. In a while, she came upon a shaggy black bear.

14 "Ah, Grandma!" he said, flexing his claws and sharpening them on a nearby rock. "How nice of you to arrive just when I'm so hungry!"

15 Grandma's heart went *dhuk-dhuk,* but she didn't let the bear see how scared she was.

16 "If you're planning to have me for lunch," she said, "that's a terrible idea. See how thin I am? I'll be a lot fatter on my way back from my daughter's house because she's such a good cook. You can eat me then, if you like."

17 "That sounds good!" said the bear, and he let her go.

CLOSE READ

Analyze Plot and Setting

<u>Underline</u> details that tell you Grandma could be in danger again.

flexing curling

Use Text Evidence

Highlight text evidence that supports an appropriate response to this question: How do you know that Grandma solved the problem of the bear planning to have her for lunch?

Analyze Plot and Setting

Underline details that help you picture the new danger that Grandma faces.

crouching bending down

18 Grandma walked into the deepest part of the jungle, *khut-khut-khut*. Suddenly she came upon a sleek, striped tiger.

19 "Ah, Grandma!" he said, crouching low and swishing his tail. "How nice of you to arrive just when I'm so hungry!"

20 Grandma's heart went *doom-doom*, but she didn't let the tiger see how scared she was.

21   "If you're planning to have me for dinner," she said, "that's a terrible idea. See how bony I am? I'll be a lot juicier on my way back from my daughter's house because she's such a good cook. You can eat me then, if you like."

22   "That sounds good!" said the tiger, and he let her go.

Use Text Evidence

Highlight text evidence that shows that the tiger believes Grandma when she says that he can eat her on her way back home.

Use Text Evidence

Highlight details that describe what kind of experience Grandma had during her visit. Use this text evidence to support an appropriate response to this question: Did Grandma enjoy her visit with her daughter?

23 Grandma reached her daughter's house. She had a wonderful time there, playing with her grandchildren and telling the neighbors all about her adventures in the forest.

24 She worked in her daughter's garden, watering, digging, and sprinkling the ground with her special fish-bone fertilizer until the vegetables grew so large that people from three villages came to admire them. She ate the delicious dishes her daughter cooked and, just as she'd told the forest animals, she grew quite plump!

25 But Grandma missed her dogs.

26 She wondered if they had guarded her garden or if they had let the mice and birds eat everything up, *kutur-kutur-kut*?

27 Finally, she told her daughter, "It's time for me to go home. Kalu and Bhulu are waiting for me, and so is my vegetable garden. The only problem is, the tiger, bear, and fox are waiting, too! And this time I won't be able to trick them with words."

28 "Don't worry!" said the daughter. "We'll come up with a plan!"

CLOSE READ

Analyze Plot and Setting

Underline the detail that describes the problem Grandma faces.

Use Text Evidence

Highlight details that describe the solution to Grandma's problem.

29   The two of them went into the garden so they could think better, and when they saw the giant gourds they knew exactly what to do.

30   The daughter picked the biggest gourd and hollowed it out. Grandma climbed in. The gourd was quite comfortable because its walls were as thick as a mattress and its rind was as tough as a rhino's hide. The daughter gave Grandma some puffed rice and tamarinds to eat on the way and stitched the top of the gourd back on tightly and sealed it with rice glue.

31   "Now no one will know it's you," she said.

32   She took the gourd to the edge of the jungle and gave it a strong push. *Gar-gar, gar-gar*! The gourd began to roll down the jungle path.

33   In a while, the gourd reached the part of the forest where the tiger was waiting for Grandma. Because he had never seen such a large gourd, the tiger didn't know what it was.

34   "What a strange creature!" he cried.

35   He sniffed around the gourd, but because it was all sealed up, the tiger couldn't smell Grandma.

Use Text Evidence

Highlight clues that tell you the solution to Grandma's problem is working.

Analyze Plot and Setting

Underline details that help you picture where Grandma is.

36   In a thin, high voice, Grandma chanted, "I'm just a rolling gourd, singing my song. Won't you give me a push and help me along?"

37   "I guess I could do that," said the tiger. "I wonder when that old woman's coming back, though. I'm getting terribly hungry."

38   It rammed the gourd with its head and sent it bouncing down the path.

39   *Daraam-daraam*, bounced the gourd.

40   "*Baap re baap*!" said Grandma. "That was close! It's a good thing that the flesh of this gourd is so soft or my bones would be shaking like the stones inside a rattle." And she ate some puffed rice and tamarinds.

41   In a while, the gourd reached the part of the forest where the bear was waiting. He, too, didn't know what the gourd was.

42   "What a strange creature!" he cried. He sniffed around the gourd, but because of the rice glue he couldn't smell Grandma.

43   Grandma chanted, "I'm just a bouncing gourd, singing my song. Won't you give me a push and help me along?"

Use Text Evidence

Highlight a detail that describes Grandma's progress on her journey.

44   "I guess I could do that," said the bear. "I wonder when that old woman's coming back, though. I'm getting terribly hungry." He gave the gourd a powerful swipe with his paw and sent it spinning down the path.

45   *Chat-pat, chat-pat,* spun the gourd.

46   "*Baap re baap*!" said Grandma. "That was close!"

47   "It's a good thing the walls of this gourd are so thick and strong or by now I'd be dizzy as a dervish." And she ate some more puffed rice and tamarind.

48 The gourd rolled and bounced and spun until it was almost at the edge of the forest.

49 *Only a little while longer*! thought Grandma.

50 Just then the gourd reached the part of the trail where the fox was waiting for Grandma.

51 "What's this now?" he cried, sniffing around the gourd.

52 Grandma chanted, "I'm just a spinning gourd, singing my song. Won't you give me a push and help me along?"

CLOSE READ

Analyze Plot and Setting

Underline details that tell you Grandma is getting close to home. Briefly explain the influence of this setting on the plot.

Analyze Plot and Setting

Underline details that describe Grandma's new conflict, or problem. Analyze this plot element by answering this question: How does this conflict move the sequence of events forward?

53   But the clever fox said, "One hundred and one times I've sneaked into villages to steal chickens, but I've never seen a singing gourd! Something odd is going on here." He grabbed the top of the gourd with his sharp, pointy teeth and shook it back and forth until the rice glue cracked and the stitches broke off. Out fell Grandma, *dhap-dhapash*!

54   "Ah, Grandma!" grinned the fox.

55   "How nice and plump you look! Whatever were you doing inside a gourd?"

56   "You caught me fair and square," said Grandma. "I guess you deserve to eat me up. But I have a request. Can I sing one last song before you start chewing on me?"

57   "Oh, all right," said the fox, drooling a little. "Just don't make it too long."

58   "I won't!" said Grandma. At the top of her voice she sang,

59   "Kalu, Bhulu, *tu-tu-tu*!

60   Kalu, Bhulu, come to me, do!

61   Kalu, Bhulu, I need you!"

Analyze Plot and Setting

<u>Underline</u> details that describe how Grandma's problem is solved. Use these details to analyze the resolution of the story.

62   Back in the village, Kalu and Bhulu heard Grandma's voice. They knew she was in danger. Quick as wind, *hoosh-hoosh*, they flew into the forest, fangs bared, growling horribly. They chased the fox away, scaring him so much that he never came back.

63   Grandma gave her dogs a big hug.

64   "Thank you, boys!" she cried. "You saved my life!"

65   *"Gheu! Gheu!"* said Kalu and Bhulu modestly.

66   "It was nothing!"

67   When she got back to her hut, Grandma was delighted to see that her garden was chock-full of vegetables. Kalu and Bhulu had done a good job!

68   She picked the freshest ones and cooked a delicious pot of khichuri, with lentils and rice, cauliflowers and peas, and shiny white potatoes as big as your fist.

69   And together they ate it all up.

CLOSE READ

Vocabulary in Context

Context clues are words and sentences around an unfamiliar word that help readers understand the word.

Use a context clue beyond the sentence to determine the meaning of *modestly*.

<u>Underline</u> the context clue that supports your definition.

Develop Vocabulary

In traditional tales and other forms of fiction, authors use precise words to describe the action and setting. These precise words help readers create pictures in their minds to better understand the plot.

My TURN Write a vocabulary word from the word bank that matches what the author is describing. Then complete the other two columns.

Word Bank

fierce   baring   swipe

Vocabulary Word	What the Author Is Describing	This word helps me know more about . . .	What I Picture
baring	the fox showing his teeth	how scary the fox must seem to Grandma.	large, sharp, pointy teeth
	what the bear does with his paw		
	jungle animals		

Check for Understanding

My TURN Look back at the text to answer the questions.

1. How can the reader tell that *Grandma and the Great Gourd* is a traditional tale?

2. Why does the author include words that imitate sounds?

3. How is the fox similar to and different from the other animals that Grandma meets?

4. Why is it important to the story for Grandma to meet the fox on her way back home? Briefly analyze this plot element.

Analyze Plot and Setting

The **setting** is when and where a story takes place. The **plot** is the sequence of events in the story, including the problem and resolution. A story's setting often affects the plot. Analyze a story's plot and setting to help you better understand the text.

1. My TURN Go to the Close Read notes in *Grandma and the Great Gourd* and underline parts that help you analyze the plot and setting.

2. **Text Evidence** Use text evidence you underlined to support an appropriate response in the chart.

Beginning	Middle	End
Setting:	Plot:	Setting:
". . . in a little hut at the edge of the village, next to a deep, dark jungle."		
Explain the influence of this setting on the plot.	Explain the influence of the conflict on the plot.	Explain the influence of this setting on the plot.
Grandma must travel through the dangerous jungle to visit her daughter.		

44

Use Text Evidence

While reading, readers look for **text evidence** that supports their understanding. Examples of text evidence may include direct quotations, details, examples, or events from a story.

1. **My TURN** Go back to the Close Read notes and highlight text evidence that relates to either the plot or setting. Consider how this evidence suggests what might happen in the story.

2. **Text Evidence** Use some of your highlighted text to show what the evidence suggests about the story's plot.

Text Evidence	What This Evidence Suggests
". . . we'll listen for you. If you get in trouble, just call for us."	Grandma's dogs will save her when she is in the jungle.

Reflect and Share

Talk About It When Grandma leaves her daughter's house, she hides inside a gourd to travel through the jungle. Think about the other forms of travel that you have read about this week. What other forms of travel might Grandma have used to get home? Use examples from the texts to support your response.

Ask Relevant Questions When having a discussion, it is important to ask questions that are relevant, or related, to the topic.

- ◎ Ask questions to clarify something that you do not understand.
- ◎ Ask questions to better understand someone else's thoughts or ideas.

Use these sentence starters to guide your questions to make sure they are relevant:

What did you mean when you said . . . ?

What evidence makes you think that . . . ?

Weekly Question

How do people travel in different environments?

Academic Vocabulary

Related Words are words that share roots or base words but can have different meanings.

Learning Goal

I can develop knowledge about language to make connections between reading and writing.

My TURN For the words listed below,

1. **Group** related words in the first column.

2. **Write** the base word, which is the word that the related words share.

3. **Use** a print or online dictionary to find the meaning of the base word. Write the definition in your own words.

competed	resolve	competition
custom	occasional	solve
occasion	organization	customize
disorganized		

Related Words	Base Word	Definition of Base Word

Syllable Patterns

Syllable Pattern VC/CV words have two consonants in the middle of them. The vowel sound in the first syllable is often short. Each syllable in a VC/CV word ends in a consonant. That means that each syllable is closed.

Divide VC/CV words between the two consonants, such as pen / cil and bar / ber. Doing this will help you read a VC/CV pattern word.

My TURN Read each VC/CV word. Remember that the first syllable will often have a short vowel sound because it is a closed syllable. Divide each word into syllables.

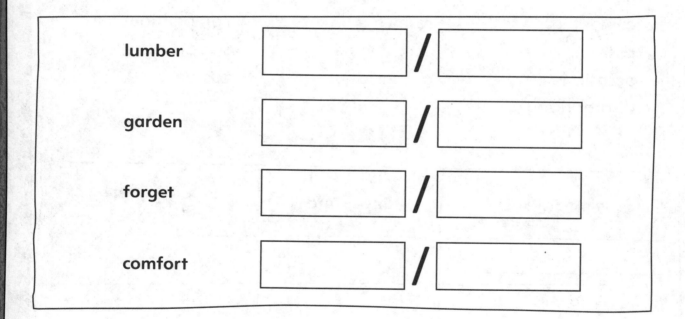

lumber   [ ] / [ ]

garden   [ ] / [ ]

forget   [ ] / [ ]

comfort   [ ] / [ ]

High-Frequency Words

High-frequency Words are words that you will see often in texts. Read these high-frequency words: *table* and *north*.

Read Like a Writer

Authors use **figurative language** to achieve a specific purpose. Figurative language gives words a meaning beyond their usual definitions, so authors use it to make their writing come alive. In a **simile**, an author compares two unlike things that are alike in at least one way. Similes include a comparison word, such as *like* or *as*.

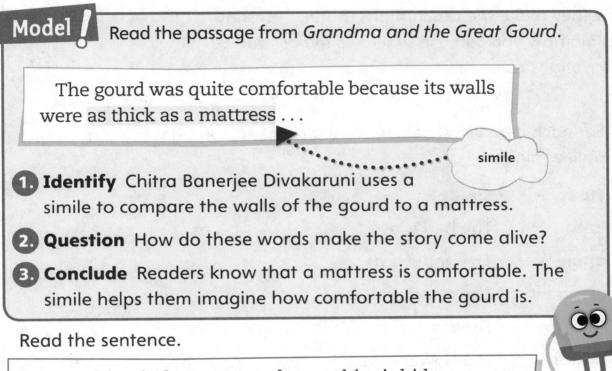

Model ! Read the passage from *Grandma and the Great Gourd*.

> The gourd was quite comfortable because its walls were as thick as a mattress . . .

simile

1. Identify Chitra Banerjee Divakaruni uses a simile to compare the walls of the gourd to a mattress.

2. Question How do these words make the story come alive?

3. Conclude Readers know that a mattress is comfortable. The simile helps them imagine how comfortable the gourd is.

Read the sentence.

> . . . and its rind was as tough as a rhino's hide.

My TURN Follow the steps to analyze simile.

1. Identify Chitra Banerjee Divakaruni uses a simile to

compare the _____ to _____ .

2. Question How do these words make the story come alive?

3. Conclude Readers know that a rhino's hide is _____

The simile helps readers imagine _____ .

Write for a Reader

Writers use figurative language to make their writing more interesting. A simile is one way a writer achieves this specific purpose.

Use a simile to compare two unlike things!

My TURN Describe how Chitra Banerjee Divakaruni uses similes in *Grandma and the Great Gourd* and how they make the descriptions more interesting. Explain how you can use similes to make your descriptions come alive.

1. For each item listed below, write a simile to compare it to an unlike thing.

Item	Simile
bed	The bed is as _____ as _____ .
apple	The apple is as _____ as _____ .
elephant	The elephant is as _____ as _____ .
train	The train is as _____ as _____ .
flower	The flower is as _____ as _____ .

2. Write about two friends walking to school. Use similes to describe what the friends see, hear, smell, taste, or touch along the way.

_____

_____

_____

_____

_____

Spell Words with the VC/CV Pattern

Syllable Pattern VC/CV words have two consonants that divide two of the syllables, with a vowel before the first of the two consonants and a vowel after the second of the two consonants. The words can be divided between these two consonants. This can help you remember how to spell VC/CV pattern words.

My TURN   Sort the words by the number of syllables.

SPELLING WORDS		
basket	mustard	cosmic
subject	compact	disgust
lesson	absent	fantastic
traffic		

Two syllables   **Three syllables**

_____ _____ _____

_____ _____ _____

_____ _____ _____

_____ _____ _____

High-Frequency Words

High-frequency words should be studied so you can remember how they are spelled. Write each high-frequency word on the line.

table _____

north _____

Simple Sentences

A **simple sentence** expresses a complete thought. It has a subject and a predicate. The subject is who or what the sentence is about. The predicate includes a verb and tells what the subject does or is. A subject and verb must agree. This means a singular subject takes a singular verb. A plural subject takes a plural verb.

Sentences begin with a capital letter and end with a period, question mark, or exclamation point.

Who or What (subject)	Action or State of Being (verb)	Simple Sentence (with subject-verb agreement)
Clay	sleep	Clay sleeps late.
The cat	chase	The cat chases a mouse.
They	like	They like the zoo.

My TURN Edit this draft to make sure that each simple sentence expresses a complete thought and shows subject-verb agreement. Add missing words, capital letters, and punctuation as needed.

Leah walk her dog, Bo. It starts to rain. run home. Bo see a giant mud puddle. rolls in it. then Bo gets up. He off the mud This covers Leah with. She is angry.

Personal Narrative

A **personal narrative** is a true retelling of an event or memory in the writer's life. Personal narratives use the pronouns *I*, *me*, or *mine*. Like fiction stories, personal narratives have a developed setting and a sequence of events.

My TURN　Use a personal narrative you have read to fill in the chart.

WHO?

Who is the narrator? What did you learn about the narrator?

WHERE AND WHEN?

Where do events take place? When do events take place?

WHAT HAPPENS?

What happens? What is the problem? How is the problem solved?

Narrator

The main person in a personal narrative is the **narrator**. The narrator's purpose is to share a special memory or experience. Narrators reveal their thoughts and feelings when they recount the events in their narrative. For example, they may include details to show they are joyful, disappointed, or angry.

My TURN Think about a personal narrative you have read. Record the narrator's thoughts and feelings.

Title: Narrator:	
Thoughts	**Feelings**

As you read, notice details about the narrator's thoughts and feelings.

Setting and Sequence of Events

Like fiction, personal narratives have a **setting**. The setting can affect the events. The **sequence of events** includes a beginning, middle, and end.

My TURN Work with a partner. Read a personal narrative from your classroom library. Use details from the text to answer the questions. Discuss your ideas.

Setting
Where and when does the story take place?

Sequence of Events
What is the problem?
What happens first?
What happens next?
What happens at the end?

Brainstorm and Set a Purpose

When writing personal narratives, writers often **brainstorm**, or make a list of ideas. Brainstorming can help you focus on a **topic**, or what you are writing about. It can also help you determine a **purpose**, or why you are writing, and an **audience**, or the people who will read your writing.

Ideas to Write About	Focus on My Topic	Focus on One Moment
◐ a family trip ◐ my summer vacation	◐ going to a park ◐ going to the lake	◐ hiking a new trail ◐ catching my first fish

My TURN Think about important events in your life. Brainstorm a topic, purpose, and audience for your personal narrative.

My narrative is about _____

_____.

My purpose is to _____

_____.

My audience is _____

_____.

WRITE WITH A PURPOSE

☐ I will write about something important that happened to me.

☐ I will tell interesting details about something I want my audience to know.

☐ I will tell my audience my thoughts and feelings.

Use this checklist to organize your draft.

Plan Your Personal Narrative

One way to plan your personal narrative is to freewrite. Quickly, write down all of your ideas for a personal narrative. Do not stop to fix spelling or grammar yet. After a short time, reread what you wrote. Then choose your best ideas to include in your personal narrative.

My TURN Freewrite in the chart. Recount your experience to your Writing Club. Speak clearly, and include all appropriate or relevant facts and details.

MY TOPIC

I could write about the time when . . .

My Thoughts and Feelings	Setting	Plot
I could tell my thoughts and feelings by . . .	My story takes place . . .	The main events I will include are . . .

INTERACTIVITY

FRIENDS

How good to lie a little while
And look up through the tree!
The sky is like a kind big smile
Bent sweetly over me.

The sunshine flickers through the lace
Of leaves above my head,
And kisses me upon the face
Like Mother, before bed.

The Wind comes stealing o'er the grass
To whisper pretty things;
And though I cannot see him pass,
I feel his careful wings.

So many gentle Friends are near
Whom one can scarcely see,
A child should never feel a fear,
Wherever he may be.

Imagine yourself in this place.
What do you see, hear, smell,
taste, and touch?

Where is this place?
What can you do here?

Weekly Question

How do different cultures relate to their environments?

Freewrite How do you work and play in the place where you live? Write your ideas quickly.

Learning Goal

I can learn more about traditional tales and infer theme in a folktale.

Spotlight on Genre

Folktale

A **folktale** is a type of traditional tale that comes from a particular country or culture. Folktales were told long ago and passed down from generation to generation. Folktales include

- **Characters,** usually people, animals, or nonliving things that act like humans
- **Problems,** often between people or people and animals
- **Plots** that involve a problem and solution
- A **theme,** or central message

Establish Purpose The **purpose,** or reason, for reading a folktale is often for enjoyment. You might also read to learn about beliefs and values of a different culture.

Notice what is important to the people who tell the folktale.

My **PURPOSE** _____

_____

_____

_____

TURN and TALK With a partner, discuss different purposes for reading *Why the Sky Is Far Away.* Establish your purpose for reading this text.

Folktale Anchor Chart

CHARACTERS

Easily recognized characters, such as a helpful fairy or a talking animal

PROBLEMS

Goals are easy to recognize: to find a prize, to marry the prince, or to overcome evil.

PLOTS

Repetition of efforts, often three times, leads to success.

Mary-Joan Gerson feels a strong connection to other cultures. She learned about Nigerian folktales while in the Peace Corps, an agency that helps people around the world who are in need of food, housing, and education. She has also written *Fiesta Feminina*, a book about seven strong Mexican women.

Why the Sky Is Far Away

Preview Vocabulary

As you read *Why the Sky Is Far Away*, pay attention to these vocabulary words. Notice how they provide clues to the theme.

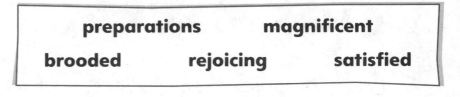

preparations		magnificent
brooded	rejoicing	satisfied

Read

Establish your purpose for reading this **folktale**. Follow these strategies when you read the folktale for the first time.

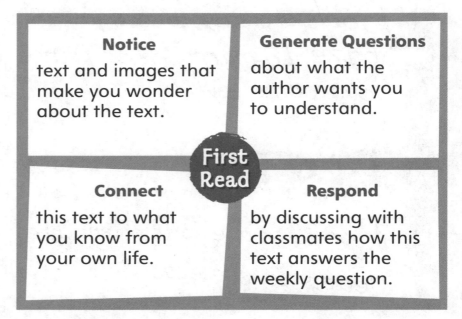

Notice text and images that make you wonder about the text.

Generate Questions about what the author wants you to understand.

First Read

Connect this text to what you know from your own life.

Respond by discussing with classmates how this text answers the weekly question.

A NIGERIAN FOLKTALE

WHY THE SKY IS FAR AWAY

retold by Mary-Joan Gerson
illustrated by Carla Golembe

AUDIO

ANNOTATE

Ask and Answer Questions

Highlight details that help you ask and answer a question about why the sky is important to the people.

1   In the beginning, the sky was very close to the earth.

2   In that time, men and women did not have to sow crops and harvest them. They did not have to prepare soup and cook rice. The children did not have to carry water from the stream or gather sticks for the fire. Anybody who was hungry just reached up, took a piece of sky, and ate it. It was delicious, too. Sometimes the sky tasted like meat stew, sometimes like roasted corn, and sometimes like ripe pineapple.

3   There was very little work to do, so people
spent their time weaving beautiful cloth,
carving handsome statues, and retelling tales
of adventures. And there were always festivals
to prepare for. The musicians practiced, the
mask makers carved their masks in secret,
and everywhere the children watched the
preparations in wonder.

4   The king of the land was called the *Oba,* and his court was magnificent. At the royal palace was a team of servants whose only work was to cut and shape the sky for ceremonies.

5   But the sky was growing angry because people were wasteful. Most often they took more than they could possibly eat and threw the leftovers onto garbage heaps.

6   "I am tired of seeing myself soured and spoiled on every rubbish bin in the land," brooded the sky.

7   So one morning at sunrise, the sky turned very dark. Thick black clouds gathered over the Oba's palace, and a great voice boomed out from above.

8   "Oba! Mighty one! Your people have wasted my gifts. I am tired of seeing myself on heaps of garbage everywhere. I warn you. Do not waste my gifts any longer, or they will no longer be yours."

9   The *Oba*, in terror, sent messengers carrying the sky's warning to every corner of the land. In every village, people were told about the sky's unhappiness. The children were warned never to take a piece of sky unless they were truly hungry.

CLOSE READ

Infer Theme
Underline sentences that help you infer the theme, or central message, of the folktale.

10   People were very, very careful—that is, for a while. . . . Then the time arrived for the greatest festival of the year. It was the festival that celebrated the power of the *Oba*.

11   The most important palace dancers performed all through the night, and the *Oba* himself, in ceremonial robes, danced for his subjects.

12   By the fifth day, there was rejoicing in every home and on every street. The *Oba* knew, though, that with the dancing and merriment, people might forget the sky's warning. So he made sure no one took more sky than he or she absolutely needed.

CLOSE READ

Ask and Answer Questions

Highlight a detail that states the purpose of the festival. Use this detail to generate questions about the festival as you read. Then use text evidence to answer your questions and deepen your understanding of the text.

Infer Theme

Underline text evidence that suggests that the *Oba* is worried about the people eating too much sky. Use this evidence to infer a theme of the folktale.

rejoicing actions and feelings of great happiness

Vocabulary in Context

Use context clues within and beyond the sentence to determine the meaning of *craved* in paragraph 13.

Underline the context clues that support your definition.

satisfied happy or pleased

13   Now, there was a woman in this kingdom who was never satisfied. She could barely move when she wore all the weighty coral necklaces her husband had bought her, but she still craved more necklaces. She had eleven children of her own, but she felt her house was empty. And most of all, Adese loved to eat.

14   On the very last night of the celebration, Adese and her husband were invited to the *Oba's* palace. There they danced and danced and ate well past midnight.

15   "What an evening it was," Adese thought later, standing in her own garden again. "How I wish I could relive tonight—the drumming I heard, the riches I saw, the food I ate!" She looked up at the sky and, hoping to taste again the cocoyams and meat stew the sky had offered, she took a huge piece to eat. She had only finished one-third of it when she could swallow no more.

16   "What have I done?" wailed Adese. "I cannot throw this away. Otolo!" she screamed, calling her husband. "Come and finish this piece of sky for me." Her husband, exhausted from dancing all night and stuffed with the sky he had eaten at the *Oba's* palace, could take only two bites.

17   "Wake the children!" screamed Adese. Now, the children had spent all night at a masquerade and party after their dinner, and most of them were still too full to even nibble at their mother's piece of sky.

CLOSE READ

Infer Theme

Underline details that suggest the reason why Adese takes more than she needs from the sky.

Ask and Answer Questions

Highlight details that describe how Adese tries to solve the problem. Use these details to ask and answer a question that helps you deepen your understanding of the folktale and its theme.

Infer Theme

<u>Underline</u> a sentence that helps you infer the reason why Adese throws away the piece of sky.

18 The neighbors were called, and the neighbors' neighbors were called, but Adese still held in her hand a big chunk of sky. "What does it matter," she said finally, "one more piece of sky on a rubbish heap." And just to make sure it didn't matter, she buried the leftover in the garbage bin at the back of her house.

19 Suddenly the ground shook with thunder. Lightning creased the sky above the *Oba's* palace, but no rain fell.

20 "Oba! Mighty one!" boomed a voice from above. "Your people have not treated me with respect. Now I will leave you and move far away."

21 "But what will we eat?" cried the *Oba*. "How will we live?"

22 "You must learn how to plow the land and gather crops and hunt in the forests," answered the sky. "Perhaps through your own labor you will learn not to waste the gifts of nature."

CLOSE READ

Infer Theme

Underline sentences that help you infer the theme of the folktale.

Ask and Answer Questions

Highlight details that you can use to ask and answer a question to better understand how the actions of one person can affect everyone.

23   No one in the land slept very well that night. The rising sun uncovered the heads of men and women and children peering over rooftops and through windows, straining to see if the sky had really left them. It truly had. It had sailed upward, far out of their reach.

24   From that day onward, men and women and children had to grow their own food. They tilled the land and planted crops and harvested them. And far above them rested the sky, distant and blue, just as it does today.

AUTHOR'S NOTE

25   This story is at least five hundred years old. It was first told in Bini, the language of the Bini tribe of Nigeria, which has existed for more than eight hundred years. The Bini people live today, along with many other tribes, in what is now the country of Nigeria. How interesting it is that the Bini people long ago began teaching their children to respect the earth and sky. Today we are very concerned about caring for our planet. We now see, as the wise Bini did then, that the future of nature and its gifts rests in our own hands.

Develop Vocabulary

In folktales, authors use words to communicate ideas about characters and events. Vivid words contribute to the theme, or central message.

My TURN Complete each sentence with a word from the word bank. Then write what the word describes and an idea about a character or event that the word helps communicate.

Word Bank

brooded   **satisfied**   **rejoicing**   **magnificent**   **preparations**

Vocabulary Word	Tells About . . .	Idea the Word Helps Communicate
___Satisfied___ means "pleased."	Adese	Adese wants more. She is not pleased.
_____ means "activities to get ready for something."		
_____ means "worried."		
_____ means "very wonderful."		
_____ means "actions and feelings of great happiness."		

Check for Understanding

MyTURN Look back at the text to answer the questions.

1. What are three details from the text that help you identify this story as a folktale?

2. What is a logical argument that you can develop to explain why the author included the Author's Note?

3. What conclusion can you draw from the following sentence? *"Wake the children!" screamed Adese.* Cite text evidence.

4. What connections can you make between the plot of the folktale and messages about greed and wastefulness?

Infer Theme

The **theme,** or central message, of a story is what the author wants the reader to learn or understand about life. Usually, the theme is not directly stated. Instead, the reader must **infer** the theme, or make an educated guess. It is important to recognize, or distinguish, that a theme is different from a topic, or what the story is about.

1. **My TURN** Go to the Close Read notes in *Why the Sky Is Far Away* and underline the parts that help you infer theme.

2. **Text Evidence** Use some of the parts you underlined to complete the chart.

Topic of Folktale:
Natural resources

Theme of Folktale:

Key Detail	Key Detail	Key Detail
"Your people have wasted my gifts.... Do not waste my gifts any longer, or they will no longer be yours."		

Ask and Answer Questions

Before, during, and after reading, readers can ask and answer questions about a text and its theme. Asking and answering questions about a text helps readers gain information and deepen their understanding of the text.

1. **My TURN** Go back to the Close Read notes and highlight key details that help you ask and answer questions about the theme.

2. **Text Evidence** Use your highlighted text to complete the chart.

Question I Could Ask	Key Detail That Helps Me Answer the Question
How did the people depend on the sky?	"Anybody who was hungry just reached up, took a piece of sky, and ate it."

Reflect and Share

Write to Sources Think about the cultures you have read about this week. How are they similar and different? How are the lessons they teach relevant to your personal experiences? How are they relevant to all cultures? Use these questions to help you write a response.

Demonstrate Understanding When you are writing, it is important to demonstrate, or show, that you understand the ideas in the texts you are writing about. Before you start writing, ask and answer questions about the texts you read.

- What makes the cultures similar or different?
- What lessons or experiences seem to be important?

Next, ask and answer questions about your own experiences.

- What lessons have I learned that are similar to the ones I have read about this week?
- How are the characters similar to or different from me?

Then, use text evidence and your own experiences to write your response on a separate sheet of paper.

Weekly Question

How do different cultures relate to their environments?

Academic Vocabulary

Learning Goal

I can develop knowledge about language to make connections between reading and writing.

Synonyms and Antonyms A **synonym** is a word that has the same or nearly the same meaning as another word. An **antonym** is a word that means the opposite of another word.

 For each word,

1. Write the definition.

2. Choose two synonyms or antonyms for the word.

3. Use your glossary or a print or online dictionary to check your work.

---

competition, n. _____

Synonyms: _____

Antonyms: harmony, agreement

solve, v. _____

Synonyms: figure out, answer

Antonyms: _____

organization, n. _____

Synonyms: _____

Antonyms: disorganization, disorder

Inflected Endings

Inflected Endings Most plural nouns end in -s. Words that end in *sh*, *ch*, *tch*, *s*, *ss*, or *x* need to have -*es* added to them to make them plural. These letters add another syllable to the word, as in the word *boxes*. To make words that end in a consonant and the letter *y* plural, change the *y* to an *i* and then add -*es*.

Read each singular and plural noun below.

Singular Noun	Plural Noun
wish	wishes
fox	foxes
watch	watches
glass	glasses
strawberry	strawberries
baby	babies

My TURN Write the plural form of each noun.

1. sky _____

2. statue _____

3. watch _____

High-Frequency Words

High-frequency words are words that you often see in texts. Read these high-frequency words: *story*, *draw*.

Read Like a Writer

Authors use graphic features to achieve specific purposes, such as helping readers picture an idea or identify the mood.

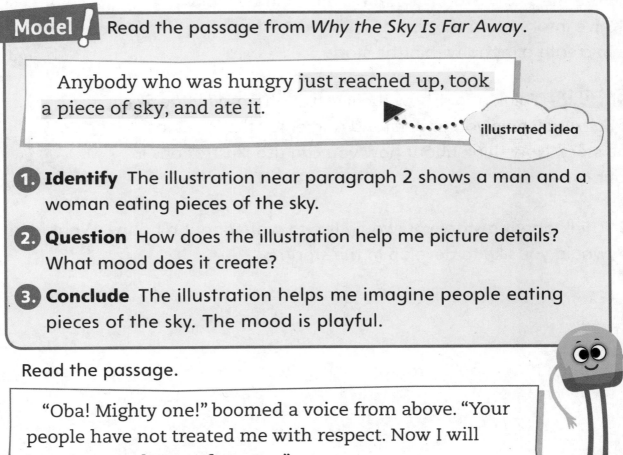

Model Read the passage from *Why the Sky Is Far Away*.

Anybody who was hungry just reached up, took a piece of sky, and ate it.

illustrated idea

1. **Identify** The illustration near paragraph 2 shows a man and a woman eating pieces of the sky.

2. **Question** How does the illustration help me picture details? What mood does it create?

3. **Conclude** The illustration helps me imagine people eating pieces of the sky. The mood is playful.

Read the passage.

"Oba! Mighty one!" boomed a voice from above. "Your people have not treated me with respect. Now I will leave you and move far away."

My TURN Follow the steps to analyze the passage.

1. **Identify** The illustration near paragraph 20 shows

_____.

2. **Question** How does the illustration help me picture details? What mood does it create?

3. **Conclude** It helps me picture _____

_____. The mood is _____.

Write for a Reader

Graphic features add visual details.

Writers use graphic features, such as illustrations, to achieve specific purposes. They may help readers picture the story. Graphic features may show details or give information that is not in the text. They may help create a mood within the story.

My TURN Think about how the illustrations in *Why the Sky Is Far Away* help you understand and enjoy the ideas in the story. Now think about how you can use illustrations in your own story.

1. Think about a story you would like to write about a hobby. What idea would you like to develop in the story?

_____

_____

2. Explain how this illustration will help readers understand your idea.

_____

_____

_____

3. Write about a hobby. Include details that tell about it. Then draw the illustration on another sheet of paper.

_____

_____

_____

Inflected Endings

Inflected Endings Many singular nouns change to a plural form by adding the ending *-es* or *-ies*. The spelling of some nouns changes when the ending is added.

Example:
Change *y* to *i*: baby → babies

My TURN Sort the words by their endings.

SPELLING WORDS		
inches	spies	pennies
pitches	fries	families
dishes	cities	faxes
glasses		

–ies

_____

_____

_____

_____

_____

–es

_____

_____

_____

_____

_____

High-Frequency Words

High-frequency words are common and appear frequently. Write the following high-frequency words on the lines.

story _____

draw _____

Subjects and Predicates

A complete simple sentence has a subject and a predicate. The **subject** tells who or what the sentence is about. The **complete subject** includes all the words in the subject.

The **predicate** tells what the subject does or is. The **complete predicate** includes the verb and the words after the verb that state something about the subject. The verb in the predicate must agree with the noun in the subject. This means a singular subject takes a singular predicate. A plural subject takes a plural predicate.

Complete Subject	Complete Predicate
The <u>men</u> on the farm	<u>plant</u> crops.
My best <u>friend</u>	<u>practices</u> before the game.
Her favorite <u>artists</u>	<u>display</u> work in the museum.

My TURN Edit this draft of simple sentences for subject-verb agreement.

Our whole town watch the Tigers play soccer. The Saturday games is always exciting. The fast players score the most goals. The many fans yell and claps.

Develop an Engaging Idea

Writers retell an interesting or memorable experience in a personal narrative. They use relevant details, or details closely related to the story, to focus their ideas. These details allow readers to share in the writer's experience and understand the writer's thoughts and feelings.

My TURN Think about stories you have read with engaging ideas. Use the chart to list relevant details that develop engaging ideas.

Questions	Details
What makes the idea interesting?	
What does the author see?	
What does the author hear?	
What does the author feel?	
What does the author taste or smell?	
What does the author do?	

My TURN Use the questions to develop and focus engaging ideas with relevant details in your own personal narrative.

Narrator

Narrators tell about an event with their actions, words, thoughts, and feelings. A narrator can help authors focus their writing by providing readers with relevant details. These details allow the reader to connect with the narrator's experience.

My TURN Read the passage. Then complete the chart by listing relevant details that tell about the narrator.

> I had butterflies in my stomach when I walked into my new school. I thought of my friends and how we played on the beach. We swam. We collected seashells. Now I felt homesick. All eyes were on my flowery skirt and long, black ponytail. I wanted to run, but I squeaked out a "hello."

Narrator Looks Like	Narrator Thinks and Feels	Narrator Likes to Do

My TURN Edit one of your own drafts of your personal narrative. Focus your writing to include relevant details that develop engaging ideas.

Focus on details that relate to the event you want to tell.

Compose a Setting

Relevant details help writers structure their writing so readers can picture in their minds the setting, or where and when the events happen. To develop the setting in an engaging way, writers use craft such as relevant, sensory details to help readers experience the way things look, sound, smell, taste, or feel.

My TURN Read the passage. Then complete the chart.

Last year on a sunny day, my family and I took a hike at Stone Park. We followed a maze of trails that wound through dense forests. Birds whistled overhead. Then, BOOM! A loud crack quickly followed. I looked at my map and spotted a shelter nearby. Raindrops as big as eggs fell on our heads as we ran. Safe inside, we watched giant raindrops splash outside and breathed in the sweet smells of wet earth.

Details About the Time	Details About the Place	Relevant, Sensory Details (Craft)

My TURN As you compose your personal narrative, use craft to add relevant, sensory details that help structure your writing and develop an engaging setting.

Problem

One of the most important genre characteristics of a personal narrative is the problem, or the conflict that must be resolved. The sequence of events tells the order in which events leading up to the conflict happened. Narrators share a problem they have had and write details to describe why the problem is meaningful.

My TURN Read a personal narrative from your classroom library. Look for the genre characteristic of the problem, or conflict, as you read. Then complete the chart.

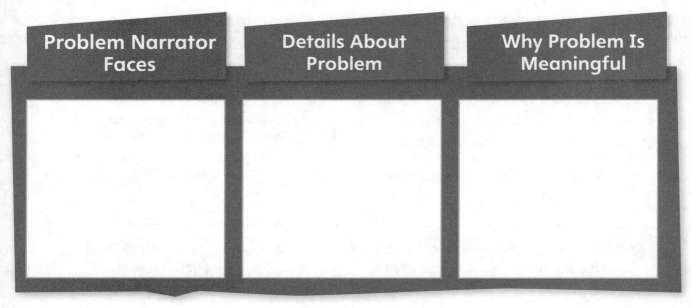

Problem Narrator Faces	Details About Problem	Why Problem Is Meaningful

My TURN As you compose your personal narrative, be sure to include the genre characteristic of a problem. In one of your own drafts, add details about the conflict to help your readers understand why it is meaningful.

Strong details help make the conflict real.

Resolution

The resolution brings the narrative to a satisfactory ending. It may tell how the problem is solved and how the narrator changed because of the experience. A strong ending ties a personal narrative together. A strong ending might be a surprise, a summary, a reflection, a question, or a lesson learned.

Original ending: We lost the game and I went home.

Stronger ending: We lost the game, but the courage I learned from my teammates was more important than winning.

My TURN Write a resolution for this personal narrative. Then share it with members of your Writing Club. Follow agreed-upon rules for discussions, including talking politely with others.

As I washed the dishes, I stared out the kitchen window. I saw something out of the corner of my eye. I turned off the sink faucet and looked more closely. There! I saw it again! My neighbor's new puppy had escaped and ran across our backyard. I raced to the door, hoping I would not be too late to catch it. "Here doggy, doggy, doggy," I coaxed.

_____

_____

_____

_____

_____

My TURN In one of your own drafts, edit your resolution to make it stronger.

INTERACTIVITY

Exploring a RAINFOREST Environment

Rainforests are hot and humid places with much rain. Rainforest environments are found in Africa, Asia, South America, Central America, and Australia.

The FOREST FLOOR: The floor is very dark, so few things can grow. Giant anteaters can find plenty of food here.

Weekly Question

How can an environment affect lives and relationships?

The EMERGENT LAYER: This layer has trees up to 200 feet tall. Here, many birds and butterflies fly around the tallest treetops.

The CANOPY LAYER: This is where treetops make a leafy roof over the rainforest floor. Many birds and animals, including toucans, live in this thick growth of branches.

The UNDERSTORY LAYER: Only a little sun can reach this layer, so the plants and trees here grow large leaves. Many of the large cats, such as jaguars and leopards, climb and hunt here.

Turn and Talk Take turns reading aloud sections of the diagram with a partner. Discuss the main idea and key details of each section. Describe how your food, clothing, home, or activities would change if you lived in a rainforest environment.

I can learn more about themes concerning *environments* by analyzing characters in realistic fiction.

Realistic Fiction

Realistic fiction is a made-up story that could possibly happen in real life. It may include imaginary **characters** who act like real people in real situations.

The characters in realistic fiction may be

- **Major characters:** the main character and other characters who are important to the plot
- **Minor characters:** characters who do not play an essential role in the plot events

Characters may narrate as a character within the story (first-person point of view) or narrate as an observer (third-person point of view).

Watch for ways the characters change in a realistic fiction story!

TURN and TALK Discuss with a partner how realistic fiction is similar to and different from a traditional tale. Use the Realistic Fiction Anchor Chart to help you compare and contrast the genres. Take notes on your discussion.

My NOTES

_____

_____

_____

_____

_____

REALISTIC FICTION ANCHOR CHART

PURPOSE:
- To entertain or tell a story

TEXT STRUCTURE:
- Events are often told in order, or in sequence.
- The story has a beginning, middle, and end.

ELEMENTS:
- The setting is a real place or a place that could be real.
- Characters behave like real people.
- The plot includes events that could happen in real life.

Andrés Pi Andreu traveled through Cuba to learn about his environment. He explored mountains and caves, hidden beaches, and valleys. Ciénaga de Zapata was one of those places. Andrés lived there for a month in a town called Mosquito!

Cocoliso

Preview Vocabulary

As you read *Cocoliso*, pay attention to these vocabulary words. Notice how they provide clues about the characters and help you understand the story.

dream	amazing
bored	discovery	proud

Read

Establish a purpose for reading **realistic fiction**, such as reading to find out what the title means. Follow these strategies when you read this realistic fiction text the first time.

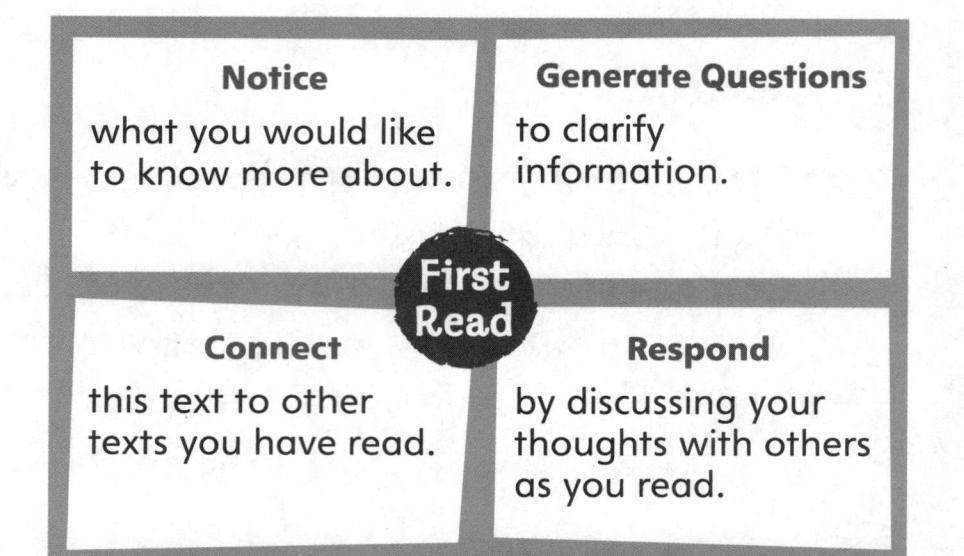

Notice what you would like to know more about.

Generate Questions to clarify information.

First Read

Connect this text to other texts you have read.

Respond by discussing your thoughts with others as you read.

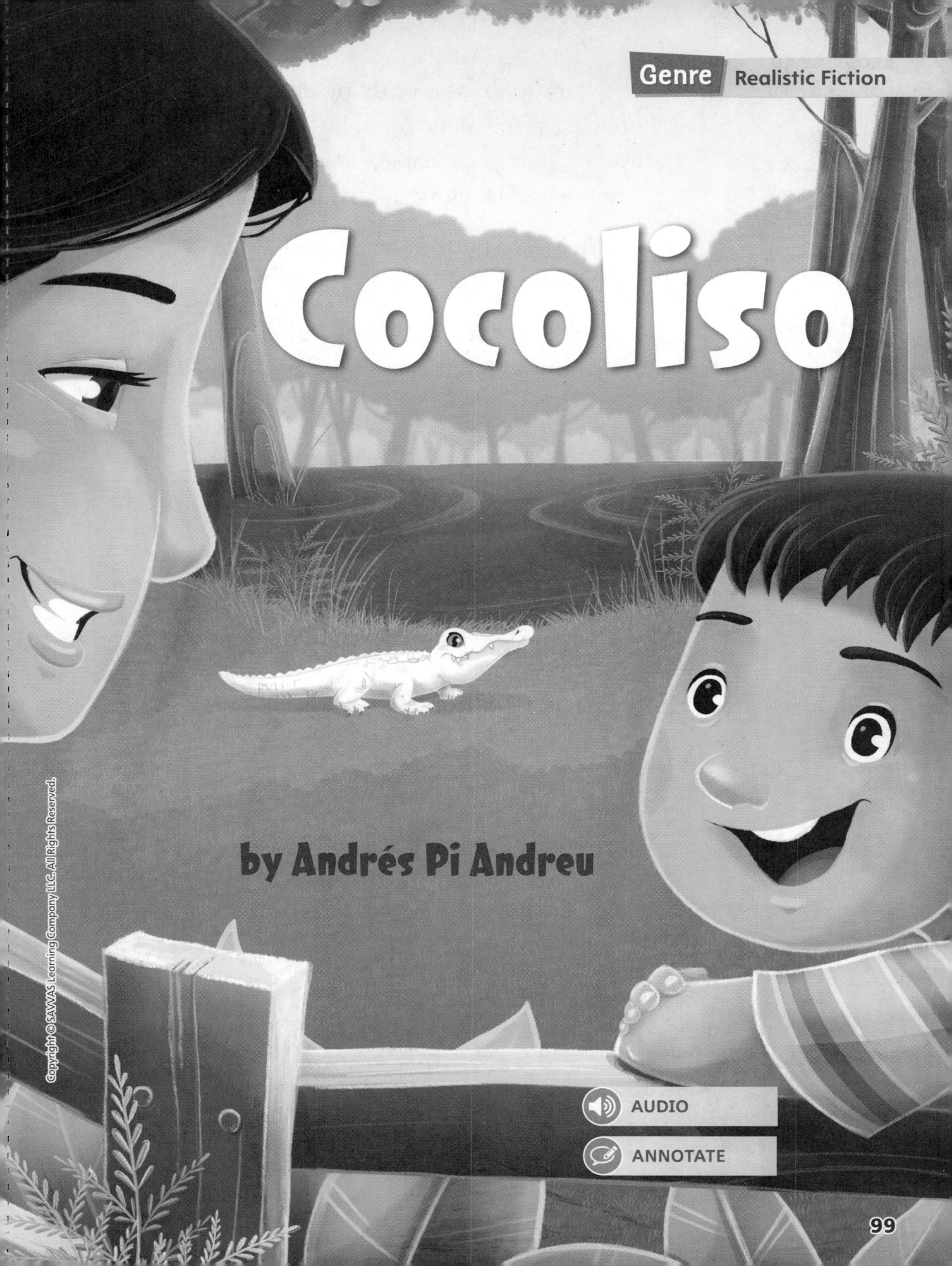

Genre Realistic Fiction

Cocoliso

by Andrés Pi Andreu

AUDIO

ANNOTATE

Analyze Characters

Underline details that help you explain the relationship between the characters Alejandro and Papi.

dreams has a desired goal or purpose

1 Alejandro dreams of flying. He dreams of being an airplane pilot. But Alejandro lives in the Ciénaga de Zapata, a swamp in western Cuba. The Ciénaga is far from any city or town.

2 "We live so far from an airport," sighs Alejandro to Papi.

3 "One day, Ale," says Papi with a smile, using Alejandro's nickname. "One day, you will fly."

4   Mama and Papi work in the Ciénaga as park rangers.

5   They often sit with Alejandro on their porch and watch the sunlight dance on the water. They listen to the hum of insects and the sweet songs of the birds. His parents teach Alejandro about the swamp.

6   "We have fifteen different kinds of mammals here," says Mama.

7   "And the *zunzuncito*! The smallest bird in the world," says Papi. "The Ciénaga is so amazing."

8   "If I could fly," sighs Alejandro, "*that* would be amazing."

Analyze Characters

Underline details that suggest how Alejandro gets along with his parents.

amazing causing great wonder or surprise

Make Inferences

Highlight text evidence about Alejandro's thoughts and feelings. Use this evidence to make and support an inference about how Alejandro feels about his home.

bored not interested in something

9   Alejandro smiles as the tiny hummingbird floats by his nose, but he is thinking of another place.

10   "When are we going to Cienfuegos?" he asks. He wants to go to the big city to visit the airport there.

11   "Soon, Ale," Papi always says, but "soon" never comes.

12   Alejandro is bored now. He jumps down from the porch.

13　"Where are you going?" asks Mama.

14　"To the Crocodile Clinic," he answers, "to see the doctor."

15　"OK, but don't take any shortcuts. Take the safe way, please!" Papi warns.

16　Alejandro has learned a lot from Mama and Papi. He knows the sound of the crocodiles and the song of the ferminias. He knows the shadow of a long-tailed hawk from the shadow of a whistling duck. He knows how to stay safe.

Analyze Characters

Underline details that reveal what Mama and Papi have taught Alejandro.

Analyze Characters

Underline details that you could use to explain the relationship between the major character, Alejandro, and the minor character, Dr. Fernanda.

17   "I know, I know," says Alejandro, and he puts on his yarey hat and heads down the path.

18   Alejandro is off to see his friend, Dr. Fernanda. She studies Cuban crocodiles. Her clinic is the only thing in the swamp as exciting as airplanes. Alejandro loves to listen to her talk about crocodiles.

19   Dr. Fernanda is funny and helpful, and she always cheers up Alejandro.

20   Alejandro stays on the path, but he can see the gar zooming in the water on either side. The long, thin fish look like rockets! The slow shadow of a manatee startles him. It is harmless, but it is so big!

21   He talks to the giant animal in the water.

22   "When I am a pilot, I will zoom through the air," he says, "just like the gar zip through the water."

23   He puts out his arms like wings and looks up at the drifting clouds.

CLOSE READ

Analyze Characters

Underline details that suggest that Alejandro is interested in the animals in his environment.

Vocabulary in Context

Context clues are words and sentences around an unfamiliar word that help readers understand the word.

Use a context clue within the sentence to determine the meaning of *pure*.

Underline the context clue that supports your definition.

24 When Alejandro looks back down, he sees he is not alone on the path.

25 A tiny crocodile baby lies at the edge. It is not like other crocs. It is pure white, as white as a cloud.

26 "Are you hurt?" he asks.

27 Alejandro takes a step closer. Then he remembers. "Never go near a wild animal in the swamp." It is a rule he has never broken.

28 "Mama and Papi will know what to do," he says to the baby.

29 He races home to get his parents.

30   Minutes later, Alejandro returns with Mama and Papi.

31   "A white croc!" they both whisper, amazed.

32   Mama makes Alejandro stand with Papi a safe distance away from the baby. Mama looks around for the baby's mother, moving carefully. She knows that a mother croc will want to protect its baby, but there are no signs of Mama Croc.

33   "I think it's hurt!" calls Alejandro. "What could have hurt it?"

Make Inferences

Highlight details that help you make an inference about Mama's reasons for acting the way she does.

Analyze Characters

Underline details that show that Alejandro cares about animals. Use these details to briefly explain the relationship between the major characters Alejandro and Cocoliso.

34   "Without its mother, almost anything could have happened," says Papi.

35   "Poor baby. I want to help it heal. Can I keep it?" Alejandro starts to beg.

36   "No, Ale, wild animals are not pets, but Dr. Fernanda can help," says Papi. He helps Mama pick up the weak crocodile.

37   "Of course!" says Alejandro. "Let's take Cocoliso to her right now!"

38   Mama and Papi scoop up the baby into
      Mama's hat.

39   "*Cocoliso*? A flat crocodile?" Mama laughs.
      "This little guy might be unusual, but he isn't
      really flat!"

40   "No," says Alejandro. "But he looks a little flat.
      AND he is white. Cocoliso looks like a crocodile
      made of white paper!" says Alejandro.

41   Mama and Papi both laugh. It's a good
      name for this crocodile.

CLOSE READ

Make Inferences

Highlight text evidence that helps you infer and supports your understanding of how Alejandro came up with Cocoliso's name.

CLOSE READ

Make Inferences

Highlight details that suggest that Alejandro is eager to take care of Cocoliso. Use this evidence to make and support an inference about what kind of person Alejandro is.

discovery something found for the first time

42   At the clinic, Dr. Fernanda looks carefully at Cocoliso. Alejandro has many ideas for how to help.

43   "I can build him a little house with a pool. I can help him make friends with the other crocodiles."

44   "Slow down, Alejandro," laughs Dr. Fernanda. "This is a crocodile, not a little brother! One thing is for sure, though. We are all very fortunate that you found this little guy. White crocodiles are very rare, and there are only a few of them in the whole world."

45   "Then I've made a great discovery!" says Alejandro.

46 "Yes, you have," replies the doctor. "Scientists from all over will be grateful for the chance to study Cocoliso."

47 Alejandro feels proud. Suddenly, the swamp doesn't seem so boring.

48 "Maybe your name and picture will be in the newspapers in Cienfeugos!" laughs Papi.

49 "Who knows? Maybe even in the capital city of Havana!" says Alejandro.

CLOSE READ

Make Inferences

Highlight a clue that Alejandro's feelings about his home have changed.

proud feeling good about oneself or something

Analyze Characters

Look at the illustration. How does it help you understand Alejandro's character? <u>Underline</u> details in the text that support your understanding.

50   "Cocoliso and I will go to Cienfuegos to meet the scientists! Then we can watch the airplanes take off and land! We could even fly to Havana!" says Alejandro.

51   He glides around with his arms out, like an airplane. Cocoliso raises his head and watches.

52   "You'll be a pilot for sure!" says Dr. Fernanda.

53   "Oh, I don't want to be just a pilot anymore!" says Alejandro.

54 "What will you be?" asks both Mami and Papi, surprised.

55 "I still want to be a pilot. But I also want to be a scientist, just like Dr. Fernanda. I'll learn how to take care of baby crocodiles. I'll make great scientific discoveries. AND, Cocoliso and I will fly all over the world telling people about crocodiles!"

56 Cocoliso seems to laugh, opening his big mouth full of tiny teeth.

57 And Alejandro feels as if he can finally fly.

CLOSE READ

Make Inferences

Highlight a detail in the text that describes how Alejandro's parents feel when they hear that he does not want to be just a pilot anymore. What can you infer about why they might feel this way?

Develop Vocabulary

In realistic fiction, authors use descriptive words to tell about the characters, such as how they look and what they think, feel, and do. Descriptive words provide clues to understanding how characters change over the course of a story.

My TURN Add the vocabulary word from the word bank to complete the chart. Explain how the word relates to Alejandro at the beginning and end of the story, using newly acquired vocabulary as appropriate.

Word Bank		
amazing	bored	dreams

Character: Alejandro			
The author uses a word that means . . .	Vocabulary Word	In the beginning, Alejandro . . .	In the end, Alejandro changes because . . .
not interested.			
has a desired goal or purpose.			
causing great wonder or surprise.			

Check for Understanding

My **TURN** Look back at the text to answer the questions.

1. How can the reader tell that *Cocoliso* is realistic fiction?

2. What details does the author include to explain the relationships among the major and minor characters? Cite one example and explain how it shows the characters' relationship.

3. What sequence of events supports the idea that Alejandro's feelings about the swamp change? Cite text evidence in your response.

4. What details and events support the idea that finding the crocodile is the most important event in the story? Cite text evidence in your response.

Analyze Characters

Readers can learn about **characters** by analyzing their **motivations**, or reasons for acting as they do, and **traits**, or qualities, actions, and appearance. Another way to understand characters is to analyze their relationships. Readers can also use illustrations to better understand characters' thoughts and feelings.

1. **My TURN** Go to the Close Read notes in *Cocoliso* and underline details that help you analyze characters in the story.

2. **Text Evidence** Use those details to complete the chart.

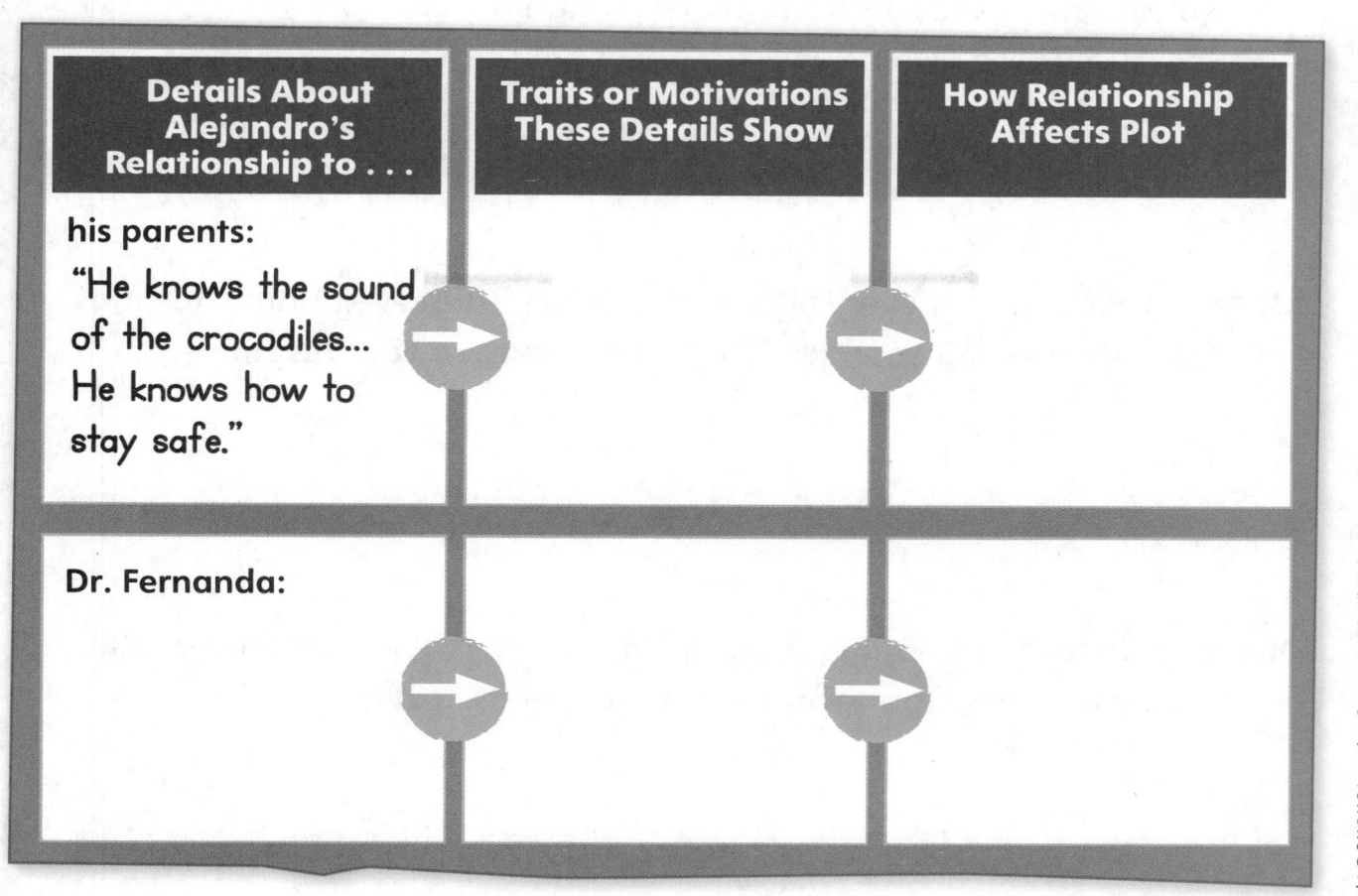

Details About Alejandro's Relationship to . . .	Traits or Motivations These Details Show	How Relationship Affects Plot
his parents: "He knows the sound of the crocodiles... He knows how to stay safe."		
Dr. Fernanda:		

How do the illustrations help you better understand Alejandro?

Make Inferences

As you read, make **inferences**, or figure out important ideas that are not directly stated in the text. Combine what you already know with evidence from the text to support your inferences.

1. **My TURN** Go back to the Close Read notes and highlight evidence that helps you make inferences about characters and their motivations, or reasons for doing what they do.

2. **Text Evidence** Use some of your highlighted evidence and what you already know to complete the chart.

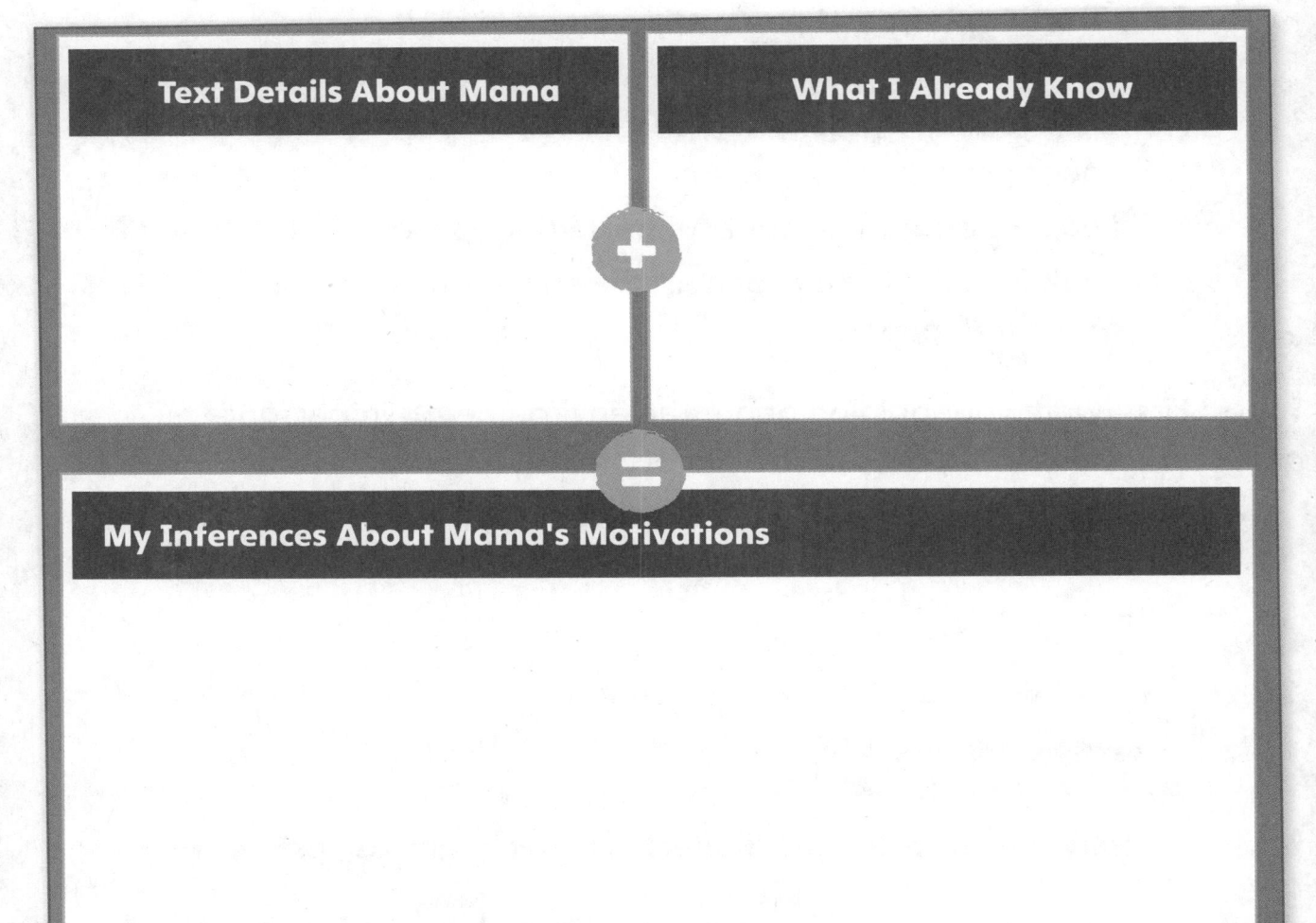

Text Details About Mama	What I Already Know

My Inferences About Mama's Motivations

Reflect and Share

Write to Sources Consider all the literary texts you have read this week. Think about the environments featured in each text. How would you describe each environment? How did the environment affect the characters and what happened in the story? Use these questions to help you write an opinion about how important an environment is to what happens in a story.

Use Text Evidence When writing an opinion, it is important to use text evidence to support your ideas.

- Look for key words or sentences that support your opinion.

- Look for quotations that support your opinion.

- Look for details that connect the environment to what happens.

First, write your opinion about the environment's importance in a story. Then choose two literary texts you read this week. Locate text evidence from each text that supports your opinion. Finally, write your opinion paragraph on a separate sheet of paper.

Weekly Question

How can an environment affect lives and relationships?

Academic Vocabulary

Learning Goal

I can develop knowledge about language to make connections between reading and writing.

Context Clues are words and phrases that help you determine the meaning of unfamiliar words. Sometimes context clues are found within a sentence or in surrounding sentences. Check the meanings of unfamiliar words in a print or digital glossary or dictionary.

My TURN For each sentence below,

1. Underline the academic vocabulary word.

2. Highlight the context clue or clues.

3. Write a brief definition of the word based on the clues. Check the meaning in the glossary.

1. To <u>solve</u> the math problem, I follow each step my teacher taught me to find the answer.
   to find an answer or solution

2. It is our custom to go on a trip every summer.

3. Millie dressed up for the special occasion.

4. The organization of words in a glossary is important. If the words are not in alphabetical order, it will be difficult to find the word you are looking for.

5. The competition for best performance at the piano recital is close because Kim and Zoe were both really good.

Base Words and Endings

A base word is the simplest form of a word. Endings may change how a base word is used or spelled. Read the highlighted words in the chart.

Base Word	+ -ed (action happened in past)	+ -ing (action is still happening)
chop	chopped (double final consonant)	chopping (double final consonant)
carry	carried (change *y* to *i*)	carrying

Base Word	+ -er (compares two things)	+ -est (compares more than two things)
large	larger (drop final e)	largest (drop final e)

My TURN Identify the word in each sentence that contains an *-ing*, *-ed*, *-er*, or *-est* ending. Underline the ending. Then write the base word.

1. Alejandro takes a step closer. _____

2. "The Ciénaga is so amazing." _____

3. "And the *zunzuncito!* The smallest bird in the world," says Papi. _____

4. "A white croc!" they both whispered. _____

High-Frequency Words

High-frequency words appear often in texts. Read these high-frequency words: *notice, slowly*.

Read Like a Writer

Authors use imagery to help readers experience how things look, sound, smell, taste, or feel. Imagery engages readers' senses and imagination.

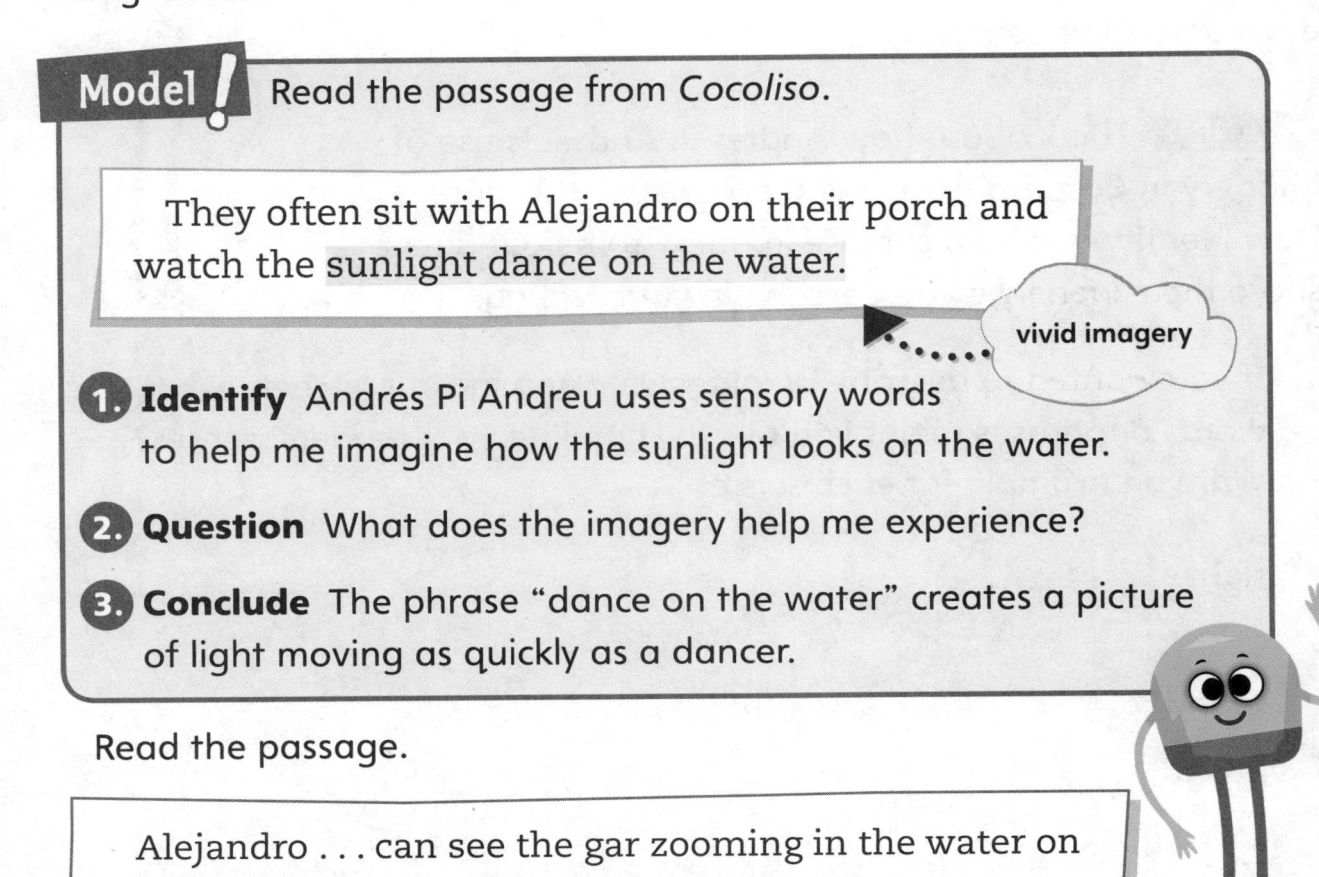

Model ! Read the passage from *Cocoliso*.

> They often sit with Alejandro on their porch and watch the sunlight dance on the water.

vivid imagery

1. Identify Andrés Pi Andreu uses sensory words to help me imagine how the sunlight looks on the water.

2. Question What does the imagery help me experience?

3. Conclude The phrase "dance on the water" creates a picture of light moving as quickly as a dancer.

Read the passage.

> Alejandro . . . can see the gar zooming in the water on either side. The long, thin fish look like rockets!

My TURN Follow the steps to analyze imagery.

1. Identify Andrés Pi Andreu uses sensory words to help me imagine

_____.

2. Question What does the imagery help me experience?

3. Conclude The phrases _____

create a picture of _____.

Write for a Reader

Writers use imagery to help their readers experience the way things look, sound, smell, feel, and taste. Different descriptive words can be used to appeal to each of the five senses.

Imagery helps readers use their senses!

My TURN   Think about how Andrés Pi Andreu's use of imagery in *Cocoliso* helped you experience the story. Now identify how you can use imagery to help readers share the experience you describe in your writing.

1. If you wanted to describe breakfast cooking in your kitchen, what words or phrases might you use to stimulate your readers' senses? Write an example for each sense.

sight _____

_____

sound _____

taste _____

_____

smell _____

touch _____

2. Write about being at a birthday party. Use imagery to help your reader experience the way things look, sound, smell, feel, and taste. Then explain how your use of imagery helps you achieve this purpose.

_____

_____

_____

_____

Spell Base Words and Endings

Base Words and Endings *-ing, -ed, -er, -est* combine to form new words. The spelling of some base words changes when endings are added to form the new words.

Examples:

Drop final *e*: give → giving

Change *y* to *i*: merry → merriest

Double final consonants: brag → bragged

My TURN   Read the words. Sort the words by their endings.

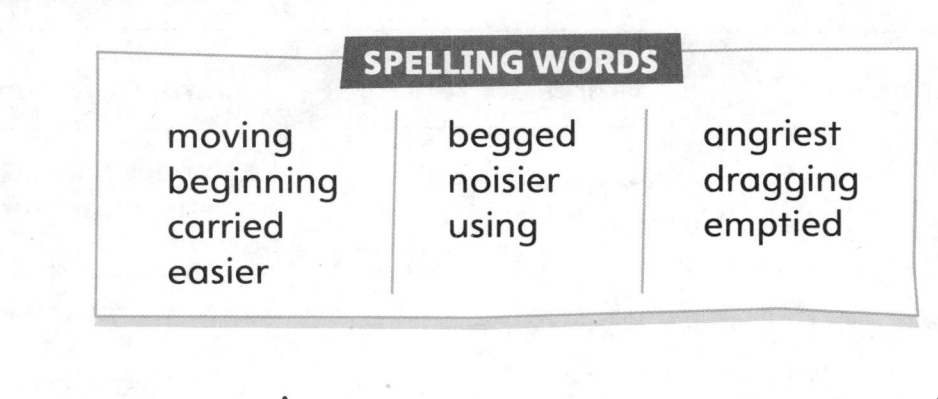

SPELLING WORDS		
moving	begged	angriest
beginning	noisier	dragging
carried	using	emptied
easier		

-ing _____   **-ed** _____   **-er** _____   **-est** _____

_____   _____   _____   _____

_____   _____   _____   _____

_____   _____   _____   _____

High-Frequency Words

Knowing how to spell high-frequency words can help you recognize them in a text. Write the following high-frequency words.

notice _____

slowly _____

Compound Sentences

A **compound sentence** is made up of two simple sentences and a comma with a coordinating conjunction (*and*, *but*, or *or*).

To form a compound sentence, follow these steps:

◎ Join simple sentences that make sense together.

◎ Add a comma before the coordinating conjunction.

◎ Use *and* to add an additional thought, *but* to add a contrasting idea, and *or* to add another choice.

◎ Make sure there is correct subject-verb agreement.

Simple Sentence	+ Simple Sentence	= Compound Sentence
I helped Mom cook.	She let me stir the batter.	I helped Mom cook, and she let me stir the batter.
Marco wants the red jacket.	His parents like the black one.	Marco wants the red jacket, but his parents like the black one.
You can buy soup.	You can make a sandwich.	You can buy soup, or you can make a sandwich.

My TURN Edit this draft by forming compound sentences with coordinating conjunctions and subject-verb agreement.

I wanted to practice the drums. Dad was napping. Mom said I could practices now in the basement. I could wait until Dad woke up. I practiced in the basement. Mom come downstairs to listen.

Compose an Introduction

An **introduction** is the beginning of a personal narrative. It gives background and details about the setting. It also sets up an event or problem and introduces the narrator. An introduction makes the reader want to keep reading.

Last fall the weather in Mason was perfect. The days were crisp, but not cold. Sadie, my best friend, invited me to go apple picking. I had never been apple picking, but it sounded like fun. Picking apples from a tree seemed dreamy. I had no idea it was hard work!

Event: apple picking
Who: the narrator and Sadie, her best friend
Setting: Mason, in the fall, in an apple orchard
Problem: hard work

My **TURN** Use the chart to organize the introduction for your personal narrative. Use your completed chart to compose an introduction to your personal narrative.

Event:

Who:

Setting:

Problem:

Develop an Event Sequence

In a personal narrative, the narrator recalls real-life **events**. Writers structure the events in a logical way. Often events are told in the order in which they happened. To show time order, use time-order words and phrases.

Examples of Time-Order Words	first, next, then, last
Examples of Time-Order Phrases	last year, later that night, one day

My TURN Read the model. Highlight the time-order words and phrases. Then write the main events in order in the graphic organizer.

> The first day of apple picking was exciting! Sadie and I filled our basket with red and golden apples. We carried the apples to a bin and emptied our baskets. The next day was not as fun. My arms were getting very sore! I carried fewer apples in my basket. That night I told Sadie, "My arms feel like rubber!" Sadie agreed that working on an apple farm is hard work.

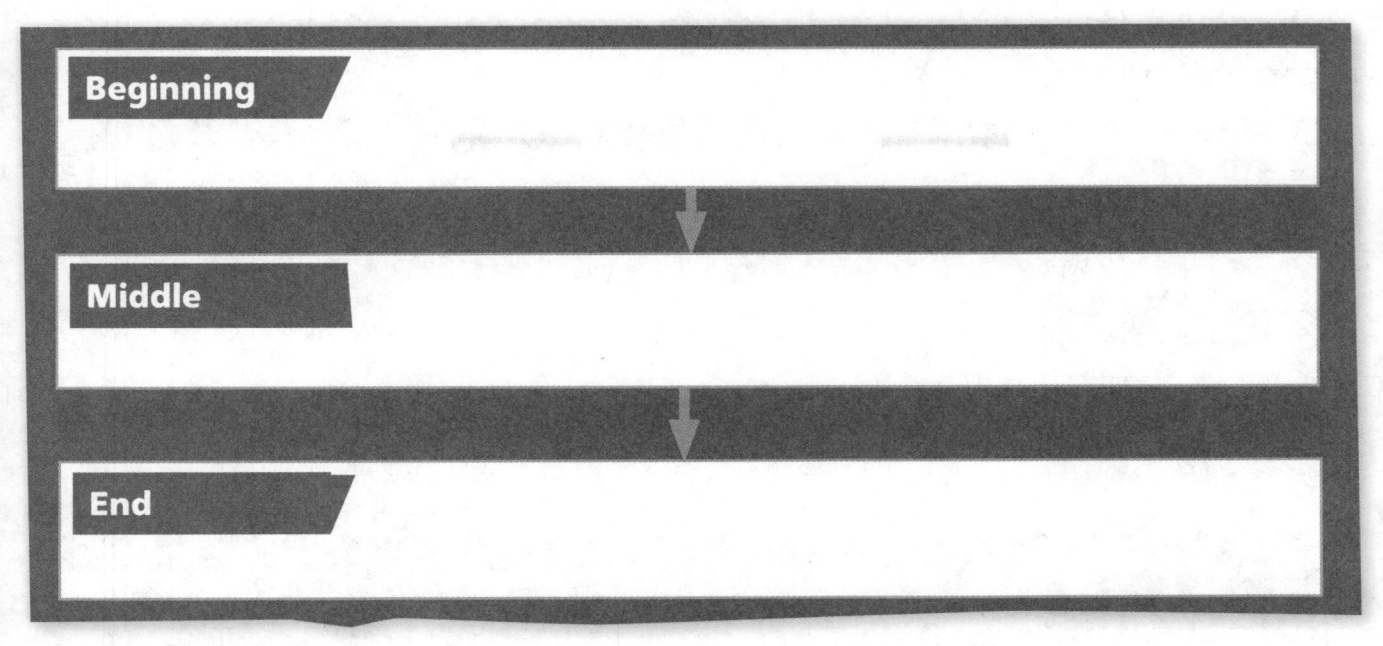

Beginning

Middle

End

My TURN In your writing notebook, use time-order words and phrases to connect events in your draft.

Develop Dialogue

Dialogue is the conversation between people in a narrative. Writers use dialogue to show a person's exact words. With dialogue, writers can show how people feel and how they react to situations. Finally, dialogue makes the narrative more interesting.

When writing dialogue:

◎ Indent and start a new line for each new speaker.

◎ Put quotation marks around the exact words spoken by a character.

◎ Capitalize the first word of what the character says.

◎ Use a comma to separate dialogue from the rest of the sentence.

◎ Use a comma after a phrase and before a quotation begins.

◎ Put punctuation inside the quotation marks at the end of what the character says.

"A dog would be a great friend," I whispered.

"We can go to the shelter on Saturday," Dad said.

I jumped up and down shouting, "Thank you! Thank you!"

My TURN Continue the personal narrative between Dad and the narrator, following the rules for writing dialogue.

_____

_____

My TURN In your writing notebook, compose some sample dialogue to include in your own personal narrative. Follow the rules for writing dialogue.

Describe Actions, Thoughts, and Feelings

To develop a personal narrative, writers describe actions, thoughts, and feelings using specific details.

My TURN   Read the model. Then answer the questions.

> I am afraid to fish in the swamp. I feel safe inside the canoe. However, when I look into the murky waters, I imagine a frightening world under the boat. Snakes slither. Alligators hunt. I smile at my uncle. I wonder if he knows how frightened I am.

1. Which words describe the narrator's actions?

2. Which words tell you how the narrator feels?

3. Which words tell you what the narrator thinks?

My TURN   In your writing notebook, compose one action, thought, and feeling to include in your own personal narrative. Then write a descriptive detail for each element.

Compose a Conclusion

A **conclusion**, or ending, of a personal narrative is usually one or two paragraphs. The purpose of the conclusion is to tie events together and to share a lesson or an inspiring moment with the reader. For example, a conclusion might explain how the experience changes the narrator.

A conclusion in narrative writing:

- summarizes the problem
- suggests a lesson learned
- provides a resolution

My TURN Complete the chart to organize your ideas. Then use the chart to help you draft a conclusion for your personal narrative.

Conclusion		
The last action, thought, or feeling that I described about my experience was . . .	What I learned from this experience was . . .	The main feeling I want to share with my readers is . . .

My TURN Identify a topic, purpose, and audience. Then select any genre, and plan a draft by brainstorming your ideas.

INTERACTIVITY

HOW DO PEOPLE
Survive in an Environment?

FLOODING When the Nile River flooded in ancient Egypt, water carried rich soil to people's land, and crops grew better. People built paths from the river to the fields so water could flow to crops during dry seasons.

HOUSING The Inuit people in the Canadian Arctic learned how to build houses from ice and snow. These igloos trap heat inside and keep people warm.

Weekly Question

What creative solutions do people come up with to survive in their environment?

TRANSPORTATION Because of the sun and wind, people can die crossing the Sahara Desert on foot. Camels can go for days without water, so people use them to travel across the desert.

Quick Write Which solution for surviving in an environment described here do you think is the most creative? Why? Use text evidence to support your response.

FARMING People living in the mountains build terraces, which are flat places that are cut into the mountains. Each terrace is a flat field for planting crops to grow food.

Learning Goal

I can learn more about themes concerning *environments* by analyzing text features in an informational text.

Informational Text

An **informational text** informs readers about a particular topic. It includes

- A **main idea,** or the most important idea in the text
- **Facts, definitions, examples,** and other **details** that provide information about the topic
- An informational **text structure,** such as cause and effect or problem and solution
- **Text features,** such as sections, tables, and graphs, that contain true or factual information
- **Images,** such as **photos or illustrations,** that explain the text or provide additional facts

Knowing the elements of informational text will help you better understand what you are reading and point you to the main ideas.

For informational text, just give me the facts!

TURNandTALK Discuss with a partner how an informational text is similar to and different from a traditional tale. Take notes on your discussion.

My NOTES

Informational Text Anchor Chart

Purpose:
To inform readers about or explain a topic

Text Structure is the way a writer
organizes ideas in a text. Informational text structures include:

Comparison and contrast
Cause and effect
Description/Definition
Problem and solution

Text Features
may be words or pictures

- Headings
- Chapters
- Index
- Glossary

- Bold words
- Table of contents
- Charts, photographs, illustrations
- Captions that explain images

Tea Benduhn
is a lawyer who is
also the author of
many children's
books. Most of
her books are
informational
texts, including
series about topics
such as food,
modern energy,
living in extreme
environments, and
living long ago.

from
Living in Deserts

Preview Vocabulary

As you read *Living in Deserts*, notice these words
and how they relate to desert environments.

	shield	**lack**
exposure	**nomadic**	**landscape**

Read

Before reading, generate questions about
information you wish to gain from the text.
Asking yourself what you want to learn about
deserts helps you establish a purpose for reading.
Follow these strategies the first time you read this
informational text.

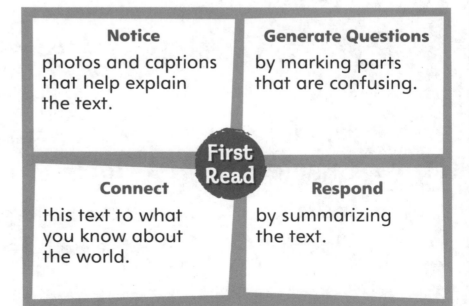

Notice
photos and captions
that help explain
the text.

Generate Questions
by marking parts
that are confusing.

First Read

Connect
this text to what
you know about
the world.

Respond
by summarizing
the text.

Living in
DESERTS

BY TEA BENDUHN

🔊 AUDIO

✏ ANNOTATE

CHAPTER 1

Welcome to the Desert

Analyze Text Features

Underline the text feature that tells you the text will be presented in a certain order.

1 The air is hot and dry. Sand blows in your face. Rocks and sand are all you can see for miles and miles. You are thirsty. You will not have much luck finding water because rain has not fallen here for more than a year. Where are you? You are in a desert!

2   A desert is an **extreme** place to live. No other place on Earth is as dry as a desert. Fewer than 10 inches (25 centimeters) of rain fall in deserts each year. The soil is dry, and rainfall can cause a **flash flood.** In the world's deserts, more people have drowned in desert rainstorms than have died from thirst.

Use Text Evidence

Highlight the detail in the text that supports what the photograph shows.

Flash floods happen when a desert's dry ground cannot soak up water quickly.

Analyze Text Features

Underline the facts in the caption and the text that the map helps you understand.

3   Deserts are almost everywhere in the world. You can find deserts in South America, North America, Asia, Australia, Africa, and Antarctica.

Deserts cover about one-quarter of all land on Earth!

ARCTIC OCEAN

EUROPE

ASIA

NORTH AMERICA

ATLANTIC OCEAN

AFRICA

PACIFIC OCEAN

ECUATOR

SOUTH AMERICA

INDIAN OCEAN

AUSTRALIA

KEY

DESERTS

SOUTHERN OCEAN

ANTARCTICA

One of the coldest places on Earth, Antarctica, is a desert!

4   Many deserts are hot. There are not enough clouds to shield the ground from the Sun's heat. One of the hottest temperatures ever recorded was in Death Valley, California. The temperature reached 132° Fahrenheit (56° Celsius)! Not all deserts are hot, however. Most of Antarctica is a cold desert. Temperatures there can be as low as −128° F (−89° C). That is way below freezing!

CLOSE READ

Analyze Text Features

Underline details in the text that support the statement in the caption.

shield protect by covering

CHAPTER 2

People of the Desert

Use Text Evidence

Highlight the detail in the text that supports the information in the chapter title.

lack the state of not having something

exposure the condition of being unprotected from severe weather, such as extreme heat

5   Deserts can be filled with danger. People can get **heatstroke** from extreme temperatures. Lack of water can lead to **dehydration.** Too much exposure to the Sun can cause sunburn. Some people, however, are able to live in deserts. To them, deserts are home.

6 For hundreds of years, people have found ways to **protect** themselves against the extreme **conditions** of deserts. They build shelters for shade during the day. They travel at night. The nomadic people of Asia's Gobi Desert move from place to place to find **resources.** They live in tent-like structures called yurts, which they carry with them.

A yurt is easy to put up, take down, and move. It will stay standing even in winds of 90 miles (145 kilometers) per hour.

Analyze Text Features

<u>Underline</u> the details in the text that the photograph helps you understand.

nomadic moving around a lot

Miners in Coober Pedy, on the edge of Australia's Great Victoria Desert, escape the Sun's heat in their underground homes. The town's name means "white man in a hole."

CLOSE READ

Use Text Evidence

Highlight details in the text that tell you more about what you can see in the photograph.

7   Different groups of people live in deserts around the world. Each group has its own way of life. They build different types of shelters to suit their ways of life. Some build homes with bricks they make from mixing mud with straw. Some people live underground! The people of Coober Pedy, Australia, dig underground rooms to make their homes.

8   Long ago, the only people who lived in deserts lived **traditional** lifestyles. Today, many kinds of people live in deserts. They use modern technology to build air-conditioned buildings and to pump water into their cities. Las Vegas, Nevada, for example, is in the Mojave Desert.

CLOSE READ

Analyze Text Features

Underline details in the text that give you more information about the photograph.

Some modern cities, such as Las Vegas, are in the middle of deserts.

CHAPTER 3

CLOSE READ

Use Text Evidence

Highlight the text details that support the chapter title by telling how people find water to survive in the desert.

Living in the Desert

9   Harsh weather and **climate** make it hard for people to live in deserts. Over many years, people have learned ways to find enough water to survive. The San people of the Kalahari Desert, in Africa, for example, know which plants store water. They also use long **reeds** to suck up water from underground. They then store the water in ostrich eggshells.

10   Most people who live in deserts live near an **oasis**. An oasis has enough water to grow crops. Many people have palm trees. A fruit called a date grows on these trees. People can also grow olive trees, wheat, and other crops for food. If an oasis is big enough, people can build villages, towns, or even cities around it.

Analyze Text Features

Underline details in the caption and text that the photograph supports.

Dates grow on palm trees. People can eat them or trade them for money or other goods.

These Tuareg people live in the Sahara Desert. They cover their faces with long, flowing cloaks. Their clothes keep sand out of their eyes, hair, mouths, and skin.

CLOSE READ

Use Text Evidence

Highlight the detail in the text that helps you understand the photograph and caption.

landscape the natural features seen in a particular area

11   Very few plants grow in deserts. Often, deserts go on for hundreds of miles of land with no shade. Strong winds blow through the **barren** landscape. A dust storm can strike at any moment without warning. Desert people wear layers of loose-fitting clothes to protect themselves from the Sun and blowing dust.

12   Some people who live in deserts do not stay in one place. The Tuareg people live in the Sahara Desert in Africa. For hundreds of years, they have traveled across the desert. They carried items for trade, such as gold and spices, from one side of the desert to the other.

Analyze Text Features

Underline the text feature that supports your understanding of why the Tuareg people raise goats.

The Tuareg people raise goats to provide milk and meat and to carry water across the desert.

Camels have often been called "ships of the desert." They can live for a long time off the fat stored in their humps.

CLOSE READ

Vocabulary in Context

Underline the context clues in the caption and the text that help you determine the meaning of the phrase *ships of the desert*.

13   For hundreds of years, many people have used camels to travel through the desert. Camels are built to survive desert weather and climate. Their thick, wooly hair protects them from the hot Sun. Their wide feet stop them from sinking in the sand. They can drink 25 gallons (95 liters) of water in minutes, and they do not need to drink again for days.

14   Fewer than one hundred years ago, many people could not cross a desert without a camel. Today, camels are less important than they once were. People now drive cars and trucks through deserts. Deserts are easier to cross today, but you would not want to get stranded! You may not get help for a long time.

Strong winds blow sand through deserts. Blowing sand makes it hard for drivers to see the road.

CHAPTER 4

People and the Desert Today

Use Text Evidence

Highlight the text details that tell you how people who live in the desert today meet their needs.

15   Every year, more people live on the edges of deserts. They cut down trees for fuel and farm the land. They bring animals, such as goats, to **graze** on the land. The areas surrounding deserts cannot support all the people who live in them. Humans use up lots of water. As people use the land, the soil loses its **nutrients** and becomes weak.

16   Most kinds of plants cannot grow in weak soil. Without plants to hold the soil in place, it can dry out and blow away in heavy winds. Dry earth can cover smaller plants and stop them from growing. Every year, more land turns into desert, and the world's deserts grow bigger. The spreading of desert edges is called **desertification.**

Analyze Text Features

<u>Underline</u> details in the text that the map helps to explain.

The yellow areas on this map show the current desert areas in Africa. The red shows areas at risk for desertification.

AFRICA

KEY

NON-DESERT AREAS

PRESENT DESERT AREAS

AREAS AT RISK FOR DESERTIFICATION

Use Text Evidence

Highlight text evidence that you could use to support an appropriate response to this question: How can pollution affect deserts and the planet?

17   Some people harm deserts. They have found valuable resources in the desert. Large companies mine deserts for precious metals, such as gold. Others drill for oil. Some nations test bombs and other weapons in deserts. Such use of deserts causes **pollution**, which can spread to the rest of the world. Pollution of the desert can harm the whole planet.

Desert mines cause pollution that can spread to other parts of the world.

Scientists hope to stop the spread of deserts by planting new crops and trees. They cover the plants with plastic covers that look like tunnels.

18   Some people, however, are trying to save deserts. **Conservation** scientists are trying to replant areas that have become desert. They build plastic covers over healthy crops, which stops plants from drying out. Some governments restrict the ways people can use the land. Other deserts are protected as national parks. Protecting deserts can help the planet.

CLOSE READ

Use Text Evidence

Highlight the detail in the text that explains why plants are covered with plastic covers.

Glossary

barren   not able to have living things grow

climate   the weather and temperature usually found in an area

conservation   having to do with careful protection of something

dehydration   extreme thirst or the state of being without enough body fluids due to lack of water

desertification   the changing of fertile land into desert

extreme   having more of something, such as heat or dryness, than we are used to

flash flood   a sudden, violent flood that occurs in heavy rainstorms

graze   feed on grass

heatstroke extremely high body temperature as a result of too much exposure to the Sun

nutrients substances that living things need to grow

oasis a place in a desert that has water

pollution human-made waste that harms the environment

protect keep safe

reeds tall grasses with long, stiff stems

resources natural substances that people can use to make their lives better

traditional having to do with a way of life and beliefs that have been in use for many generations

CLOSE READ

Use Text Evidence

Highlight the definition that describes a location where people are likely to live in the desert.

Analyze Text Features

Underline the text feature that helps you recognize a type of source you could use to find more information about deserts.

For More Information

Books

Deserts. Habitats (series). Fran Howard (Buddy Books)

Deserts. Heinemann First Library (series). Angela Royston (Heinemann)

Deserts. Learning About the Earth (series). Emily K. Green (Bellwether Media)

Deserts. Where on Earth? (series). JoAnn Early Macken (Gareth Stevens)

Index

Africa 138, 144, 147, 151

Antarctica 138–139

Asia 138, 141

Australia 138, 142

camels 148–149

climate 144, 148, 154

clothes 146

crops 145, 153

Death Valley 139

desertification 151, 154

drowning 137

Gobi Desert 141

gold 147, 152

heatstroke 140, 155

homes 142

Kalahari Desert 144

Las Vegas, Nevada 143

Mojave Desert 143

nomads 141

North America 138

oasis 145, 155

palm trees 145

plants 144, 146, 151, 153

pollution 155

resources 141, 152, 155

Sahara Desert 146–147

scientists 153

shade 141, 146

soil 137, 150–151

South America 138

storms 137, 146

Sun 139–140, 142, 146, 148, 155

thirst 136–137, 154

travel 141, 147–148

water 136–137, 140, 143, 144–145, 147–148, 150, 155

winds 141, 146, 149, 151

CLOSE READ

Analyze Text Features

Underline the index entries that might provide information about where deserts are located.

Develop Vocabulary

In informational text, look for precise words authors use to give information about a specific topic or subject. These words are called domain-specific words. Knowing their meanings will help you understand the text and use the words correctly.

My TURN Review the definition for each word from *Living in Deserts*. Then think about how each word relates to survival in a desert and place the word into the correct box in the chart.

Word Bank

shield   lack   exposure   nomadic   landscape

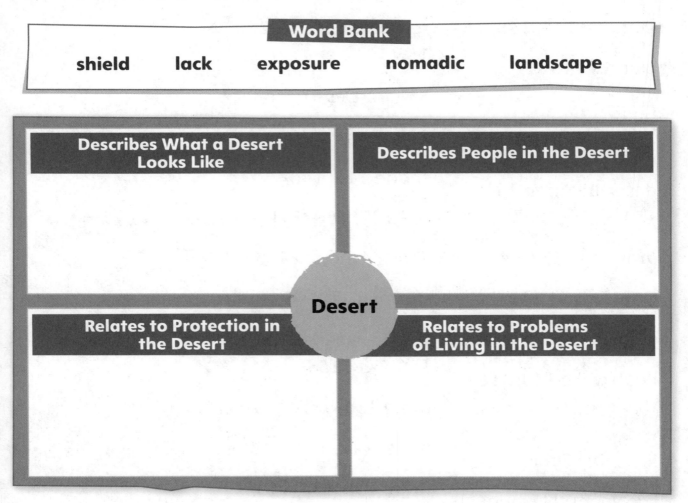

Describes What a Desert Looks Like

Describes People in the Desert

Desert

Relates to Protection in the Desert

Relates to Problems of Living in the Desert

Check for Understanding

My TURN Look back at the text to answer the questions.

1. How can the reader identify this text as informational text?

2. What is the most likely reason that the author included a glossary?

3. Compare and contrast life for people in deserts today with life in deserts long ago. Cite text evidence, and use words and phrases from the glossary in your response.

4. What information can you gather and evaluate that supports the idea that people can help save deserts?

Analyze Text Features

Text features help readers find and understand information. Examples of text features in informational texts include section headings, numbered chapters, maps, photos, captions, bold or italic text, glossaries, and lists of sources of information.

1. **My TURN** Go to the Close Read notes in *Living in Deserts* and underline details that help you analyze text features.

2. **Text Evidence** Use some of the parts you underlined to complete the chart.

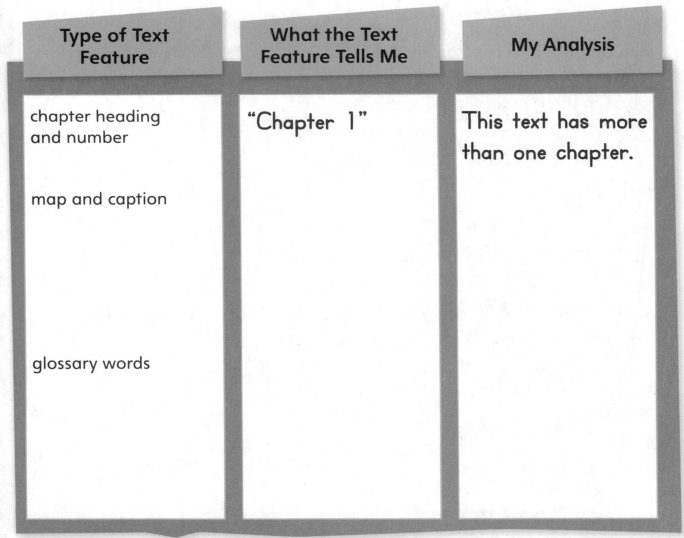

Type of Text Feature	What the Text Feature Tells Me	My Analysis
chapter heading and number	"Chapter 1"	This text has more than one chapter.
map and caption		
glossary words		

Use Text Evidence

Text evidence and text features work together in an informational text. Use both text evidence and text features to support an appropriate response to questions about a text.

1. **My TURN** Go back to the Close Read notes and highlight text evidence that works with text features in *Living in Deserts*.

2. **Text Evidence** Use some of the highlighted text to complete the chart.

Text Feature	Text Evidence	How the Feature and Evidence Work Together
photo of a flash flood	". . . rainfall can cause a flash flood."	The evidence tells what causes the flash flood shown in the photo.
the chapter title "Living in the Desert"		
photo and caption of Tuareg people		

What do the text evidence and text features help me understand about living in the desert?

Reflect and Share

Write to Sources In *Living in Deserts*, you learned about people living in an extreme environment. How do people live, work, and play comfortably in different environments? Choose two texts you read this week about environments. Then use examples from these texts to write and support a response that demonstrates your understanding of the texts.

Interact with Sources Writers interact with sources in meaningful ways, such as notetaking. Take notes to help you organize information and answer questions you have about a text. Before you write a response, think about questions you have about a text.

- ◎ Which details tell about a problem related to living in a particular environment?
- ◎ Which details tell about a solution to the problem?
- ◎ How does the solution make lives better or safer?

Take notes or underline ideas and details in at least two texts. Then use this text evidence to write your response on a separate sheet of paper.

Weekly Question

What creative solutions do people come up with to survive in their environment?

Academic Vocabulary

Figurative Language is any language that gives words a meaning beyond their dictionary definitions. One type of figurative language is simile, which compares two things using the words *like* or *as*.

Learning Goal

I can develop knowledge about language to make connections between reading and writing.

My TURN For each sentence below,

1. **Read** each sentence and underline the simile.

2. **Match** each word in the word bank with the simile that best relates to the definition of the word.

3. **Choose** two similes. Then use each simile and its related academic vocabulary word in a sentence.

WORD BANK

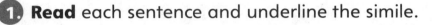

competition   solve   custom   occasion   organization

Tina always wears a yellow hat so it has become <u>as expected as the sunrise</u>. **custom**

The bookshelf looks as neat as a pin. _____

People assumed Tim was too young to win, but he is as tough as nails.

_____

Family game night is always like a party. _____

Figuring out math problems is as easy as pie. _____

Vowel Digraphs

Vowel Digraphs are two letters that spell one vowel sound. Digraphs *ee* and *ea* can spell a long *e* sound (*street, mean*). Digraphs *ai* and *ay* can spell a long *a* sound (*mail, stay*). Digraphs *ow* and *oa* can spell a long *o* sound (*glow, float*). Understanding digraphs can help you read multisyllabic words.

My TURN Read each word. Then complete the chart.

coaster	beetle	approach	reason	cattail
freezing	blowfish	playground	boating	crayon
painter	yellow	pillow	teacher	trailer

Sound	Digraph	Word
Long *e*	*ee*	**beetle**
	ea	
Long *a*	*ai*	
	ay	
Long *o*	*ow*	
	oa	

High-Frequency Words

High-frequency words are used often in texts. Read these high-frequency words: *voice, south*. Identify them when you read.

Read Like a Writer

Authors of informational texts use graphic features for the purpose of giving more detailed information about a topic.

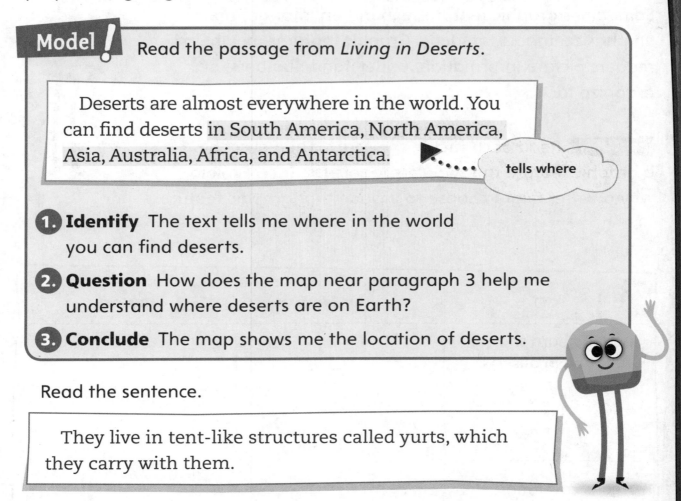

Model ! Read the passage from *Living in Deserts*.

> Deserts are almost everywhere in the world. You can find deserts in South America, North America, Asia, Australia, Africa, and Antarctica.

tells where

1. **Identify** The text tells me where in the world you can find deserts.

2. **Question** How does the map near paragraph 3 help me understand where deserts are on Earth?

3. **Conclude** The map shows me the location of deserts.

Read the sentence.

> They live in tent-like structures called yurts, which they carry with them.

My TURN Follow the steps to analyze the text.

1. **Identify** The text tells me

2. **Question** How does the photograph near paragraph 6 help me understand what a yurt is?

3. **Conclude** The photograph shows me that

Write for a Reader

Text tells, but graphic features show!

Writers use graphic features to achieve a specific purpose: to support the facts and details in the text. Sometimes graphic features expand on information or emphasize important ideas. Graphic features may help readers picture information, understand numbers, or organize facts.

My TURN Read each fact in the chart. Then describe a graphic feature that would support the fact. Explain why a writer might choose to include that graphic feature.

Fact	Graphic Feature	Reason
Some bighorn sheep are found in deserts.		
Oceans cover more than 70 percent of Earth's surface.		
After it rains, many kinds of colorful flowers may cover parts of different deserts.		

Spell Words with Vowel Digraphs

Vowel Digraphs are two vowels that combine to spell one vowel sound. The long e vowel sound can be spelled with the digraphs *ee* and *ea*. The long *a* vowel sound can be spelled with the digraphs *ai* and *ay*. The long o vowel sound can be spelled with the digraphs *ow* or *oa*.

My TURN Read the words. Sort them by their long vowel spellings.

SPELLING WORDS

owner	display	braided	agree
peaches	shadow	charcoal	maintain
asleep	dream		

Long e

ee

_____

_____

ea

_____

_____

Long a

ai

_____

_____

ay

_____

_____

Long o

ow

_____

_____

oa

_____

_____

High-Frequency Words

Write each high-frequency word on the line.

voice _____

south _____

Compound Subjects and Predicates

A **compound subject** has two or more subjects joined by the coordinating conjunction *and* or *or*. A predicate tells what the subject is or does. Two predicates joined by *and*, *but*, or *or* form a **compound predicate**.

Harsh <u>weather</u> and <u>climate</u> make it hard to live in the desert.	compound subject	The words *weather* and *climate* joined by the coordinating conjunction *and* form a compound subject.
The desert sand <u>blows</u> and <u>stings</u> your face.	compound predicate	The words *blows* and *stings* joined by the coordinating conjunction *and* form a compound predicate.

My TURN Edit this draft by combining subjects or predicates to form compound subjects and compound predicates.

Traveling in the desert can be a challenge. The hot Sun scorches. The Sun beats down on you. So, how can you travel and stay safe? People use cars to get across the desert. People use camels to get across the desert. Be sure to bring plenty of water. It pays to be prepared.

Coordinating Conjunctions

Learning Goal

I can use elements of narrative text to write a personal narrative.

A **coordinating conjunction** is a word that connects words or groups of words. Coordinating conjunctions include *and, or*, and *but*. Use *and* to add information. (I like pickles *and* tomatoes.) Use *or* to give a choice. (We can play ball *or* ride bikes.) Use *but* to show a difference. (I like popcorn, *but* she does not like it.)

A coordinating conjunction can join . . .	Example
two subjects to make a **compound subject**.	<u>Jason</u> **and** <u>his brother</u> went to the beach.
two verbs to make a **compound predicate**.	The dogs <u>sleep</u> **or** <u>play</u> outside.
two sentences to form a **compound sentence**.	<u>I made some muffins</u>, **but** <u>they were not very tasty</u>.

My TURN Rewrite the paragraph by adding conjunctions to form compound subjects, compound predicates, and a compound sentence.

Julio had fun at the baseball game. Nancy had fun at the baseball game. The crowd cheered. The crowd waved banners. Julio and Nancy wanted to buy a snack. The vendors were out of popcorn.

My TURN Edit your personal narrative for coordinating conjunctions.

Comparative and Superlative Adjectives

An **adjective** is a word that describes a noun or pronoun. A **descriptive adjective** tells how something looks, sounds, feels, tastes, or smells.

Sample Sentences	Adjective	Noun
The **little** bird flew toward the cactus. My brother listens to **noisy** music.	little noisy	bird music
I sank my toes into the **hot** sand. We ate **sweet** watermelon for dessert.	hot sweet	sand watermelon

A **comparative adjective** compares two things. A **superlative adjective** compares three or more things. Add -er to form most comparative adjectives. Add -est to form most superlative adjectives. For example: Raoul is *taller* than Ben. James is the *tallest* student in his class.

My TURN Read the paragraph. On each line, write an appropriate adjective. Then underline the correct form of the adjective in parentheses.

Lost Pines is a _____ park. The grass is (greener, greenest) there than the grass at Rolling Hills Park. The trees are quite (tall, taller), and they are some of the (older, oldest) trees in town. The park has a _____ lake too. There is also a garden with _____ flowers.

My TURN Edit your personal narrative for comparative and superlative adjectives.

Pronouns

Pronouns are words that take the place of nouns. The chart shows different kinds of pronouns.

Subject Pronouns	Object Pronouns	Possessive Pronouns
I	me	my, mine
you	you	your
he, she, it	him, her, it	his, her, hers, its
we	us	our, ours
you	you	yours
they	them	their, theirs

A **subject pronoun** functions as the subject of a sentence. (**She** read aloud.) An **object pronoun** is used after an action verb or a preposition such as *to* or *with*. (I told **him** to wait. Mandy went with **me**.) A **possessive pronoun** shows who or what owns, or possesses, something. (Maria couldn't find **her** hat.)

My TURN Complete each sentence with the correct pronoun.

1. Leo got a bike for _____ birthday.

2. Yesterday, _____ rode his bike to Jane's house.

3. "Leo, that bike looks like _____ bike," _____ said.

My TURN Edit your personal narrative for subject, object, and possessive pronouns.

Adverbs

Adverbs describe verbs and tell more about the action. Adverbs can convey time and manner. That means they can tell when or how something happens. An adverb can describe a verb, an adjective, or another adverb. Many adverbs end in *-ly*.

Manner (tells how): loudly, quietly, happily, sadly, slowly, quickly
Example: The lizard ran **quickly** over the sand. (How?)

Time (tells when): daily, weekly, yearly, always, never, now, tomorrow
Example: We take a spelling test **weekly**. (When?)

Some adverbs compare actions. To compare two actions, add *-er* to most adverbs. To compare three or more actions, add *-est* to most adverbs.

Adverb	fast	Jeff runs **fast**.
Comparative	faster	Alice runs **fast<u>er</u>** than Jeff.
Superlative	fastest	Of all the students, Bruce runs **fast<u>est</u>**.

My TURN Add an adverb to each sentence to convey time or manner.

1. We are visiting the park _____.

2. The turtles crawl _____ toward the lake to swim.

3. The ducks quack _____ as they swim.

4. The ducks swim _____ than the turtles do.

My TURN Edit your personal narrative for adverbs that convey time and manner.

172

Subject-Verb Agreement

Subjects and verbs must agree in number. Singular subjects take a singular verb. Plural subjects take a plural verb.

Most singular verbs end in -s or -es.	Rosa **helps** the teacher. The baker **mixes** the dough.
Most plural verbs do not end in -s.	The farmers **grow** corn.
Irregular verbs have their own form.	I **have** a dog, but she **has** a cat.

- A **simple subject** that includes two words, such as a first and last name, still takes a singular verb: <u>Amy Brown</u> **walks** to school.

- A **compound subject** joined by *and* takes a plural verb: <u>Amy and Tommy</u> **walk** to school.

My TURN Edit the paragraph for subject-verb agreement. Discuss the reasons for your edits politely with your Writing Club.

The desert have a variety of birds. Wrens and woodpeckers sing and chatter all day long. Some birds builds their nests in cactuses. When Stan goes to the desert, he look for hawks. They is big and easy to spot.

My TURN Edit simple and compound sentences in your personal narrative for subject-verb agreement.

 INTERACTIVITY

THE WORLD
Around Us

Natural resources help us survive on Earth. Land, water, and plants are natural resources found in an environment. A renewable natural resource can be replaced. A nonrenewable natural resource is in limited supply.

Watch this video to learn more about natural resources.

LAND: Less than one-third of Earth is land. We need land to grow food. Soil is a renewable resource, but it can wear out if overused. We know how to irrigate, or keep watered, dry land so more plants can grow.

▶ **WATCH**

"Enjoying Our Environment"

WATER: More than two-thirds of Earth's surface is water. Ocean plants make oxygen for us to breathe. Rivers, lakes, and streams are sources of fresh water for drinking.

PLANTS: Trees help keep the air clean. Trees make oxygen. Forests provide habitats for animals. Trees are a renewable resource if we replant what we use.

Weekly Question

Why should we appreciate our environment?

Turn and Talk What natural resources are discussed in the text and the video? What characteristics of each element helped you learn about the topic? Why should we be grateful for natural resources? Make connections to your personal experiences. Discuss your ideas with a partner and take notes.

Spotlight on Genre

Myth

Myths are old stories passed along by word of mouth. An **origin myth** is a type of traditional tale. An origin myth

- Explains something in nature that people who lived long ago could not understand, such as the sunrise, tides, or fire
- Often includes gods or creatures with powers

TURN and TALK How would you describe the characters and plot of a well-known origin myth you have read? Explain how you could tell that you were reading an origin myth.

Be a Fluent Reader Fluent readers read with expression. Traditional tales may contain italicized words and dialogue between characters, which you can use to practice reading with expression.

When reading traditional tales aloud,

- Raise the pitch of your voice at the end of a sentence if you see a question mark.
- Read with strong emotion when you see an italicized word followed by an exclamation point.

ORIGIN MYTH
anchor CHART

PURPOSE: to explain something about nature

CHARACTERS might be GODS, GODDESSES, or FANTASTIC CREATURES with SPECIAL POWERS.

Stories were passed down by **WORD OF MOUTH** by the people who lived long ago.

The stories helped people make sense of something in the **NATURAL WORLD** that they could **NOT UNDERSTAND.**

Nina Jaffe
loved reading folktales and myths as a child. She is an acclaimed author, teacher, and storyteller of traditional tales and has been the United States representative at the International Festival of Storytelling in the Canary Islands, Spain.

The Golden Flower

Preview Vocabulary

As you read *The Golden Flower*, pay attention to these vocabulary words. Notice how they help you visualize, or picture in your mind, the events to better understand the story.

| pouch | globe | murmuring |
| mountainside | | footpath |

Read

Establish a purpose for reading an **origin myth**, such as looking for an explanation of something in nature. Follow these strategies when you read this myth the first time.

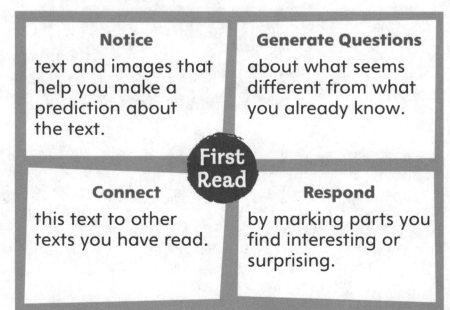

Notice text and images that help you make a prediction about the text.

Generate Questions about what seems different from what you already know.

First Read

Connect this text to other texts you have read.

Respond by marking parts you find interesting or surprising.

THE GOLDEN FLOWER

A TAINO MYTH FROM PUERTO RICO

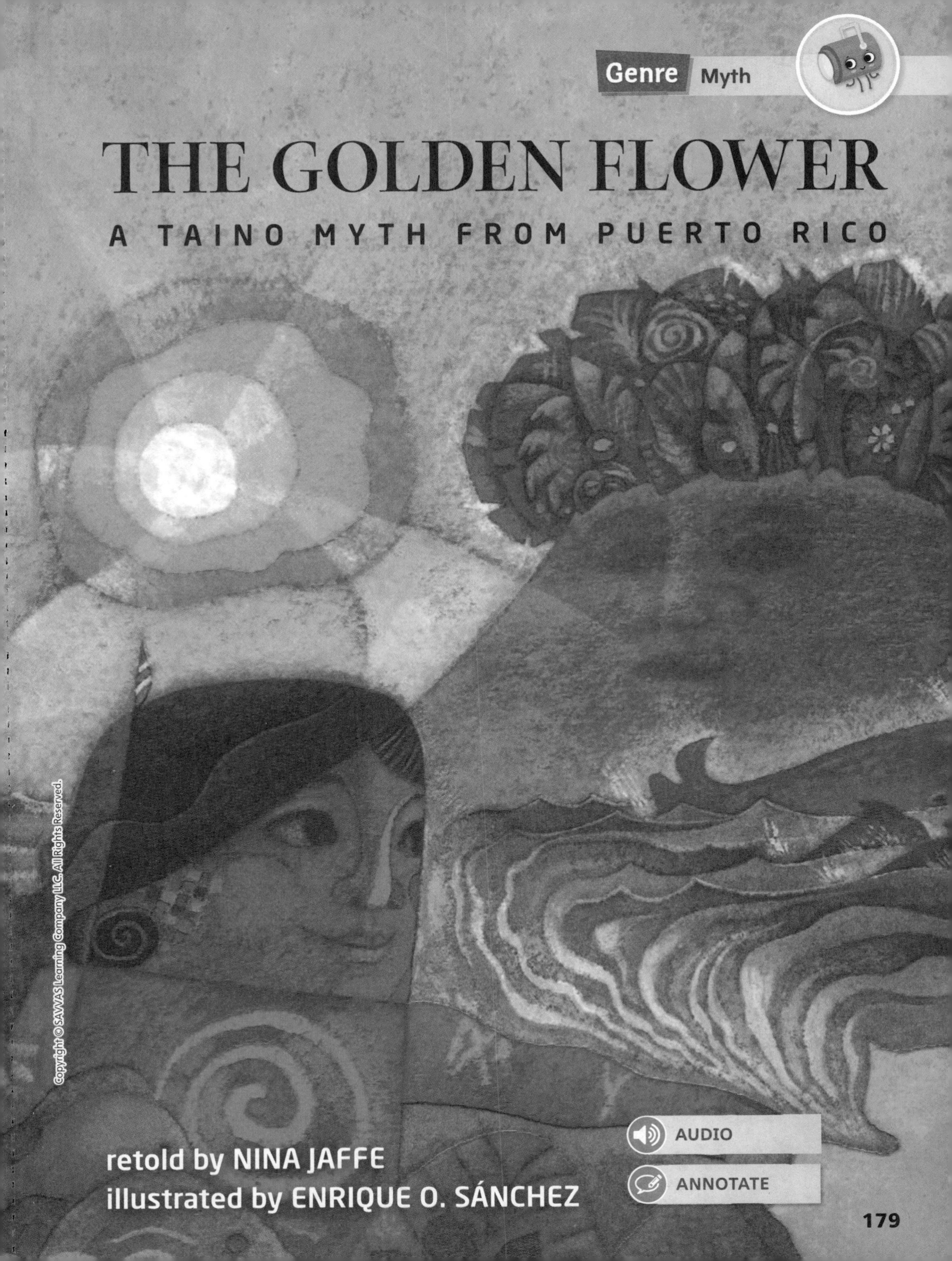

retold by NINA JAFFE
illustrated by ENRIQUE O. SÁNCHEZ

AUDIO

ANNOTATE

179

1   In the beginning of the world, there was no water anywhere on earth. There was only a tall mountain that stood alone on a wide desert plain.

2   There were no green plants. There were no flowers. All the people lived on top of this mountain.

3   One day, a child went walking on the dry land below the mountain. As he bent down over the ground looking for food, something floated by on the wind. He reached out and caught it in his hand. It was a seed. A small, brown seed. He put the seed into his pouch.

CLOSE READ

Visualize Details

Highlight words that help you create a mental image of the seed.

pouch a small bag that closes with a piece of string

Visualize Details

Highlight details that describe the seeds in the child's pouch. Use these details to create a mental image of the seeds in the pouch to deepen your understanding of the myth.

Analyze Descriptive Language

Underline details that describe the forest.

4   The next day, he went walking, and again found something as it floated by on the wind. It was another seed. Day by day, he gathered these seeds until his pouch was full. It could not hold anymore. And the child said to himself, "I will plant these seeds at the top of our mountain."

5   He planted the seeds and waited. One morning, a tiny green leaf appeared. The child watched. From under the ground, a forest began to grow high on top of the mountain.

6   All the people came to see. It was a forest of many-colored flowers, a magic garden of green leaves and thick branches. The child was happy.

Visualize Details

Highlight details that help you create a mental image of the flower that grew from the vine.

7   In the middle of the forest, at the foot of the tallest tree, there grew a vine that wrapped itself around the tree.

8   And from that vine there grew a flower more beautiful than all the rest. A bright flower with golden petals.

9   And from that flower, something new appeared in the forest. It looked like a little ball. "Look!" cried the child. "Something is growing out of the flower!"

10   As the people gathered around to watch, the ball grew larger and larger, until it became a great yellow globe that shone like the sun. Even as they walked on the dry land far below, people could see it shining on top of the mountain.

CLOSE READ

Analyze Descriptive Language

<u>Underline</u> details that describe the growing ball.

globe an object shaped like a ball

Analyze Descriptive Language

<u>Underline</u> details that describe the sounds coming from the ball.

murmuring a soft, continuous sound

11   One woman said, "If you put your ear next to the ball, you can hear strange noises coming from inside." The people listened. Strange sounds and murmuring could be heard. But nobody knew what was hidden inside.

12   The people were afraid. After that, they all stayed away. Even the child stayed away.

13   One day, a man walking on the desert plain
saw the golden ball. He said, "If that shining ball
were mine, I would have the power of the sun.
I could light up the sky, or make darkness fall."
And he ran toward it, climbing up the rocky
mountainside.

14   On the other side of the mountain, another
man saw the shining globe, and he also said,
"I want that thing for myself. It will give me
great powers." He, too, began to run. Each one
climbed quickly. Each one found a footpath that
led to the tree.

CLOSE READ

Vocabulary in Context

The word *desert* can be
a verb that means "to
leave" or an adjective
that means "dry."

Underline the context
clue that tells you that
desert is used as an
adjective in the text.

mountainside the
sloping side of a
mountain

footpath a narrow
walking path for people

Visualize Details

Highlight details that help you create a mental image of the men fighting.

Analyze Descriptive Language

<u>Underline</u> words that help you see and hear what happened to the pumpkin.

15 They both ran without stopping until they reached the shining globe at the same time. But what they found was not really a ball; it was the fruit of the golden flower: a *calabaza*— a pumpkin.

16 The two men began to fight and argue.

17 "It is mine!" said one.

18 "No, it is mine!" said the other.

19 Each man grabbed the pumpkin. They pushed and pulled. They pulled and tugged until . . .

20 . . . finally, the vine broke. The pumpkin began to roll down the mountain faster and faster, until it crashed into a sharp rock and burst apart.

Visualize Details

Highlight details that help you picture what came out of the pumpkin.

21   *Whoosh!* Waves of water poured out of the pumpkin. The water bubbled and foamed. The waves began to cover the earth, flooding the desert plain, rising higher and higher.

22   For it was the sea that had been hidden inside the pumpkin. Out came the creatures: whales, dolphins, crabs, and sunfish. All the people ran to the top of the mountain to hide in the forest of green leaves.

23 "Will the whole earth be covered?" they cried.

24 Higher and higher the waters kept rising, up the sides of the mountain.

25 But when the water reached the edge of the magic forest the little boy had planted, it stopped.

CLOSE READ

Visualize Details

Highlight a detail that helps you create a mental image of the movement of the water.

Visualize Details

Highlight details that help you create a mental image of what the people saw. How does this mental image deepen your understanding of the myth?

26   The people peeked out from behind the leaves. And what did they see? Small streams running through the trees. A beach of golden sand. And the wide open ocean, sparkling all around them.

27   Now the people could drink from the cool streams and splash in the rippling waves. Now they could gather fish from the flowing tides and plant their crops.

28　The child laughed and sang as the sun shone down and breezes blew through the green leaves and rustled the many-colored flowers. Water had come to the earth!

29　And that is how, the Taino say, between the sun and the sparkling blue sea, their island home—Boriquén—came to be.

CLOSE READ

Analyze Descriptive Language

Underline details that describe where the island is.

Fluency Read paragraphs 21–25 aloud with a partner to practice reading with expression. As you read, pay attention to the word in italics and the dialogue.

Develop Vocabulary

Authors use descriptive language in myths to tell about the setting, characters, and events. Descriptive words and phrases provide sensory details, such as how something looks or sounds, to help the reader create mental images and better understand the story.

My TURN Choose the word from the word bank that matches the dictionary definition. Then complete the last column.

Word Bank

globe	murmuring	mountainside	footpath

Word	Dictionary Definition	How the Author Uses the Word to Describe Something in the Myth
	a soft, continuous sound	
	a narrow walking path for people	
	an object shaped like a ball	
	the sloping side of a mountain	

Check for Understanding

My TURN Look back at the text to answer the questions.

1. How can you tell that *The Golden Flower* is an origin myth?

2. Why do you think the author included descriptive language about the bursting pumpkin? Cite text evidence.

3. How is the men's argument related to the creation of the people's island home? Cite evidence from the text.

4. How do the child's actions affect the people's lives? Cite text evidence.

Analyze Descriptive Language

Descriptive language, or imagery, includes words and phrases that appeal to the reader's senses. Descriptive words and phrases help the reader imagine the characters, settings, and events in a story.

1. **My TURN** Go to the Close Read notes in *The Golden Flower* and underline descriptive language in the story.

2. **Text Evidence** Use some of the parts you underlined about the pumpkin to complete the graphic organizer.

"larger and larger," "it became a great yellow globe that shone like the sun"

Pumpkin
Author's Purpose: to help readers picture the pumpkin and how it creates the sea and the island

196

Visualize Details

Visualize, or picture in your mind, **details** an author describes in the text. Descriptive language that helps you visualize deepens your understanding and enjoyment of a story.

1. **My TURN** Go back to the Close Read notes and highlight descriptive details that help you visualize parts of the story.

2. **Text Evidence** Use some of the evidence you highlighted to write descriptive details from the text and then describe what you imagine.

Descriptive Details	What I Picture in My Mind
"Waves of water poured out of the pumpkin."	water flowing out of the side of the pumpkin like water coming out of a large hose

Reflect and Share

Talk About It The Taino tell this myth about their island home to explain how the forest, flowers, water, and sea creatures came to exist. Consider all of the texts you have read in this unit. Which text do you think is most effective at describing a particular environment? Why? Use examples from the texts to support your opinion.

Make Thoughtful Comments When sharing your opinion, make sure your comments are related to the topic.

◎ Use text evidence to support your comments.

◎ Consider what others have already said.

Use these sentence starters to guide your comments:

Details that make this text the most effective at describing an environment include . . .

I agree / disagree with you because . . .

Weekly Question

Why should we appreciate our environment?

Academic Vocabulary

Parts of Speech are word categories, such as:

- **nouns:** words naming people, places, or things
- **verbs:** words that tell what something or someone is or does
- **adjectives:** words describing what nouns name
- **adverbs:** words that tell how, when, or where something happens

Words can often be used as more than one part of speech.

> **Learning Goal**
>
> I can develop knowledge about language to make connections between reading and writing.

My TURN For each sentence below,

1. **Underline** the form of the academic vocabulary word.

2. **Identify** the word's part of speech.

3. **Write** your own sentence using the same base word, but as a different part of speech. Identify the new part of speech.

Sentence	Part of Speech	My Sentence
We watched the <u>competitive</u> athletes play baseball.	adjective	I plan to compete in the race. (verb)
The reorganized supplies made it easy to find items.		
Investigators solve cases based on strong evidence.		
It is customary for Grandma to wake up early.		

Diphthongs

Diphthongs ou, ow, oi, oy A diphthong is a single vowel sound spelled with two letters. In *The Golden Flower, mountain* has the *ow* vowel sound spelled *ou. Flower* has the *ow* vowel sound spelled *ow. Noises* has the *oi* vowel sound spelled *oi. Boy* has the *oi* vowel sound spelled *oy.*

My TURN Fill in the blanks with an *ou, ow, oi,* or *oy* diphthong to form words. Then read each word aloud.

1. m<u>ou</u>ntainside

2. p ____ erful

3. c ____ nted

4. b ____ ling

5. r ____ alty

Write sentences with these words. Read each sentence aloud.

1. noises _____

2. boy _____

3. sound _____

High-Frequency Words

High-frequency words appear frequently in texts. Practice reading these words so you are familiar with them. Read these high-frequency words: *unit, figure.* Try to identify them in your independent reading.

Read Like a Writer

An author's purpose is the reason for writing a text. Readers can analyze, or figure out, the author's purpose for writing: to persuade, inform, entertain, or express something to bring about a feeling.

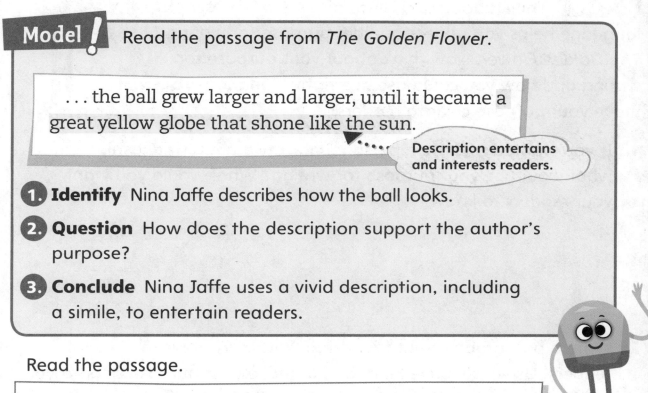

Model ! Read the passage from *The Golden Flower*.

... the ball grew larger and larger, until it became a great yellow globe that shone like the sun.

Description entertains and interests readers.

1. **Identify** Nina Jaffe describes how the ball looks.

2. **Question** How does the description support the author's purpose?

3. **Conclude** Nina Jaffe uses a vivid description, including a simile, to entertain readers.

Read the passage.

Whoosh! Waves of water poured out of the pumpkin. The water bubbled and foamed.

My TURN Follow the steps to analyze the author's purpose.

1. **Identify** Nina Jaffe describes _____.

2. **Question** How does the description support the author's purpose?

3. **Conclude** Nina Jaffe uses the word _____ to imitate a natural

sound. She describes the water with the words _____.

Her purpose is to _____.

Write for a Reader

Descriptive language entertains readers.

Writers choose elements of craft and style to achieve their purpose. They may use descriptive language, such as figurative language, to entertain readers.

My TURN Think about how Nina Jaffe's use of descriptive language helps you understand her purpose for writing *The Golden Flower*. Now think about your purpose for writing and how you could use descriptive language to make your purpose clear to readers.

1. If you wanted to write a personal narrative about friendship, what would be your purpose for writing? What would you want your readers to know?

   _____

   _____

   _____

2. Write a paragraph about friendship. Your purpose is to entertain readers. Use descriptive language to make your purpose clear to your readers.

   _____

   _____

   _____

   _____

   _____

   _____

Spell Words with Diphthongs

Diphthongs *ou, ow oi, oy* have a single vowel sound.

the *ow* sound spelled *ou*	mountain
the *ow* sound spelled *ow*	tower
the *oi* sound spelled *oi*	boil
the *oi* sound spelled *oy*	toy

My TURN Read the words. Sort them by their vowel sound. Underline the diphthong in each word.

SPELLING WORDS

thousand	bounce	annoy
shower	avoid	proud
power	appoint	fountain
enjoy		

the ow sound

_____

_____

_____

_____

_____

the oi sound

_____

_____

_____

_____

_____

High-Frequency Words

Writing high-frequency words can help you memorize the ones that do not follow regular spelling patterns. Write each high-frequency word.

unit _____

figure _____

Common and Proper Nouns

A **common noun** names a person, place, or thing. A **proper noun** names a specific person, place, or thing. Proper nouns begin with a capital letter.

Common Noun	Proper Noun
book title	*Grandma and the Great Gourd, Living in Deserts*
month	January, June, December
illustrator	Enrique O. Sánchez
teacher	Mr. Garcia, Ms. Cho
doctor	Dr. Carver
country	United States, Mexico
holiday	Thanksgiving, New Year's Day

My TURN Edit this draft by changing the underlined common nouns to proper nouns and the underlined proper nouns to common nouns. Begin each proper noun with a capital letter.

The boy walks to school. He leaves his apartment and walks down Main Street. He then walks into school. As soon as the bell rings, Mrs. Posten starts to read a book.

Edit for Legibility

Writing should be easy to read, or **legible**, so others can learn from your ideas.

To write complete words, thoughts, and answers legibly in cursive,
- form letters carefully.
- leave proper spacing between letters and words.
- write with a slight slant.
- maintain proper letter size.

My TURN Read the paragraph. Then copy it on the lines. Write legibly in cursive. Use the bulleted list to guide you as you write.

The last day of school, I ran home. The sun was shining. The air smelled like freshly cut grass. I opened the door and saw the best surprise. It was a yellow puppy!

Practice cursive writing for legibility.

Edit for Verbs

Writers edit their first drafts to make sure they are writing in the correct **verb** tense. A verb shows action or a state of being. Tense shows time.

Tense	Examples
Present-tense verbs show the action is happening now. Many regular verbs form the present tense by adding the letter *s*.	My mom <u>makes</u> pottery. She <u>sells</u> her pottery at the farmers' market.
Past-tense verbs show the action that has already taken place. Many regular past-tense verbs end in *-ed*.	I <u>walked</u> to the park with my dog. We <u>played</u> catch with a ball.
Future-tense verbs show action that will take place at a later time. To form future tense, add the helping verb *will* before the verb.	Tomorrow we <u>will play</u> soccer. I <u>will sing</u> a solo.

My TURN Read the paragraph. Replace the bold verb with a verb in the correct tense.

Yesterday, Yoli **receives** a jacket for her birthday. Yoli **will like** her new jacket. Tomorrow, she **wears** the jacket to school.

My TURN Edit one of your own drafts to check that you have used verb tenses correctly. Make corrections to verb tenses as needed.

Publish and Celebrate

Writers publish their narratives for their audience. In order to become better writers, they think about what they did well and how they can improve their writing.

My TURN Publish your narrative for your audience. Then answer the questions about your experience. Write legibly in cursive, leaving appropriate spaces between words. Consider what you did well with your writing.

What was your favorite part about writing a personal narrative?

_____

_____

_____

_____

What part of your personal narrative do you think is most interesting?

_____

_____

_____

_____

What can you improve the next time you write a personal narrative?

_____

_____

_____

_____

Prepare for Assessment

My TURN Follow a plan as you prepare to write a personal narrative in response to a prompt.

1. **Make sure you understand the prompt.**

   You will receive an assignment called a writing prompt. Read the prompt carefully. Underline what kind of writing you will do. Highlight the topic you will be writing about.

   Prompt: Write a personal narrative about a time you did something to help the environment. Describe what you did and how you felt afterward.

2. **Brainstorm.**

   List three times you have helped the environment. Highlight your favorite experience.

3. **Plan out the events in your personal narrative.**

   Put your sequence of events in order: **Beginning, Middle, End.**

4. **Write your draft.**

   Start with a strong introduction. Use vivid details to describe events. Include time-order words to put events in sequence. End with a conclusion. Write your personal narrative on a separate sheet of paper.

5. **After you finish your draft, revise and edit your personal narrative.**

   Reread your personal narrative.

Descriptive words and dialogue keep your narrative interesting!

Assessment

My TURN Before you write a personal narrative for your assessment, rate how well you understand the skills you have learned in this unit. Go back and review any skills you mark "No."

		Yes	No
Ideas and Organization	☉ I can brainstorm a special event. ☉ I can tell about the narrator and other important people. ☉ I can describe a setting. ☉ I can include an introduction and conclusion. ☉ I can organize the events in sequence.	☐ ☐ ☐ ☐ ☐	☐ ☐ ☐ ☐ ☐
Craft	☉ I can include engaging ideas. ☉ I can use descriptive language. ☉ I can include dialogue between people in the story. ☉ I can use words to show the sequence of events. ☉ I can describe actions, thoughts, and feelings.	☐ ☐ ☐ ☐ ☐	☐ ☐ ☐ ☐ ☐
Conventions	☉ I can use conjunctions to join ideas. ☉ I can use adjectives, including comparative and superlative forms. ☉ I can use subject, object, and possessive pronouns. ☉ I can use adverbs. ☉ I can write complete sentences with correct subject-verb agreement.	☐ ☐ ☐ ☐ ☐	☐ ☐ ☐ ☐ ☐

UNIT THEME

Environments

Cocoliso

by Andrés Pi Andreu

TURN and **TALK**

Connect to Theme

In this unit, you learned many new words to talk about **Environments**. With a partner, go back into each text. Find a sentence that best illustrates the academic vocabulary word. Write the sentence on the lines. Be prepared to tell why you chose that sentence.

WEEK 3

Cocoliso

custom

A NIGERIAN FOLKTALE

WHY THE SKY IS FAR AWAY

retold by Mary-Joan Gerson
illustrated by Carla Golembe

BOOK CLUB

WEEK 2

Why the Sky Is Far Away

occasion

BOOK CLUB

GRANDMA AND THE GREAT GOURD
retold by CHITRA BANERJEE DIVAKARUNI
illustrated by SUSY PILGRIM WATERS

WEEK 1

Grandma and the Great Gourd

solve

BOOK CLUB

Living in Deserts

organization

_____

_____

WEEK
4

BOOK CLUB

WEEK
5

The Golden Flower

competition

_____

_____

BOOK CLUB

Essential Question

MyTURN

In your notebook, answer the Essential Question: **How does our environment affect us?**

BOOK CLUB

Project

WEEK
6

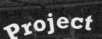

Now it is time to apply what you learned about environments in your **WEEK 6 PROJECT: A Safe Place to Play**

A SAFE Place to PLAY

Activity

What could be done to make a local park or playground safer? Compose a letter to your town's mayor or park official. Tell that person what you think could be done to improve safety in the park or playground.

RESEARCH

Research Articles

With your partner, read "What Makes a Safe Playground?" to generate questions you have about your research project. Then make a research plan for writing your letter.

1 **What Makes a Safe Playground?**

2 **Getting Outside**

3 **Discovering Great Smoky Mountains National Park**

Generate Questions

COLLABORATE Generate three questions you have after reading the article "What Makes a Safe Playground?" Share your questions with the class.

1. _____

2. _____

3. _____

Use Academic Words

COLLABORATE In this unit, you learned many words related to the theme of *Environments*. Work with your partner to add more academic vocabulary words to the chart. If appropriate, use these words in your letter to the mayor or park official.

Academic Vocabulary	Word Forms	Synonyms	Antonyms
competition	competitions compete competitive _____	contest struggle match _____	teamwork support _____
solve	solved solving solution _____	figure out crack unravel _____	question wonder _____
custom	customs customary customer _____	habit practice usual way _____	novelty _____ _____
occasion	occasions occasional occasionally _____	event function celebration _____	
organization	organize organizing organizations _____	order arrangement grouping _____	clutter disarray disorder _____

I Claim It!

People can write **argumentative texts** to give their opinion on a topic. They start by identifying the audience they are trying to reach, and then write to convince that audience to agree with their opinion. The opinion statement is also called the claim of the argument. When reading an argumentative text, look for

My **opinion** is my point of view. It is the way I see things.

- an introduction that states the topic and opinion, or claim
- reasons that support the claim and
- a conclusion that wraps up the information.

RESEARCH

COLLABORATE With a partner, read "Getting Outside." Then, answer the following questions about the text. Discuss your answers with your partner.

1. What is the writer's claim?

_____

_____

2. What is one reason the writer gives to support the claim?

_____

_____

3. Who is this article written for? How do you know?

_____

_____

Plan Your Research

COLLABORATE Before you begin researching parks and playgrounds, plan your research. Use the activity to do research for your letter, including finding relevant information from different types of sources.

Elements of an Argumentative Letter	Research Plan
OPINION An opinion is a point of view on a topic. **Example:** I believe pets can make us happy and healthy.	What information will help me form my opinion? _____ Sources: _____ My opinion: _____
REASONS Once you have formed your opinion, identify reasons that support your opinion and convince the reader. **Examples:** 1: Pets make us more active. 2: Pets help to keep us healthy.	What information will support my opinion and convince the reader? _____ Sources: _____ Reason 1: _____ Reason 2: _____

With your partner, brainstorm some possible ways that you can strengthen your opinion or reasons.

FACT-FINDING in the FIELD

Research is a careful study to find and learn facts. It is also used to collect evidence, or proof of something. **Field research** is done in person in a natural surrounding. It is helpful to do field research because it allows you to identify and gather relevant information and gain firsthand knowledge. You can then show understanding of the information you gathered.

EXAMPLE Sam and his dad want to ask the mayor to turn an empty lot into a community garden. They went to the lot to do field research. They took pictures. To show their understanding of how to improve the land, they drew a plan of the garden they want. What information would you add to their research?

Taking photos helps you to remember what you saw.

Making a sketch will help you organize and plan ideas.

COLLABORATE Ask an adult to take you and your partner to the park or playground you want to improve. Take photos and write notes to identify and gather information and evidence. Use that evidence to suggest improvements that could be made to the park or playground. With your partner, discuss ideas from your notes and photos that will be important for your letter.

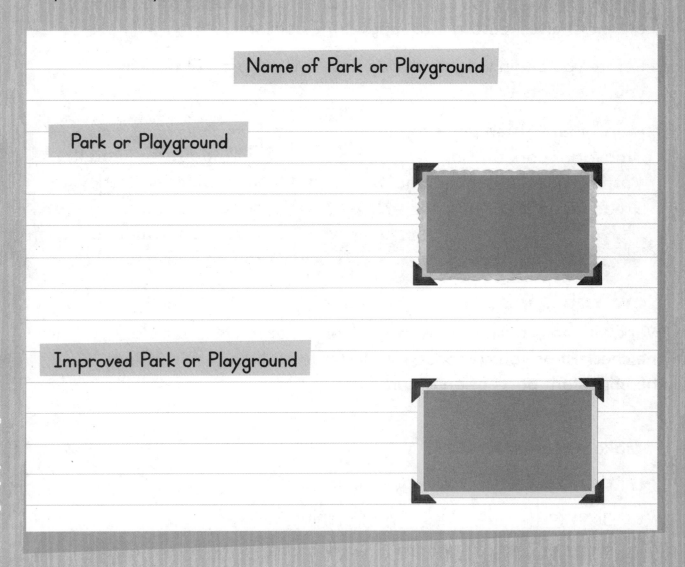

Name of Park or Playground

Park or Playground

Improved Park or Playground

Discuss your research results. How did the field research help to support your opinion? Do you need to add more specific information?

My POINT of VIEW

People write **argumentative texts** to convince others to think or act in certain ways. An argumentative letter, such as the one to the mayor or park official, expresses an opinion, or makes a claim, about a topic. It gives reasons that support the opinion.

Before you begin writing, decide how you will present or deliver your message. Will you

- mail your written letter to the mayor or park official?
- attend a town meeting and read aloud your letter there?

> **COLLABORATE** Read the Student Model. Work with your partner to recognize the characteristics of argumentative texts.

Now You Try It!

Work with your partner to write your argumentative letter. Use the checklist as you compose your letter to make sure you include the important parts of an argumentative letter.

Make sure your letter

- ☐ clearly expresses your opinion, or claim.
- ☐ gives reasons to support your opinion.
- ☐ states evidence found from field research.
- ☐ uses linking words, such as *because*, *therefore*, *since*, or *for example*, to help support your opinion.
- ☐ includes a strong conclusion that will convince readers.

Student Model

Dear Mayor Larkin,

The vacant lot on Wells Street should be turned into a community garden. The lot is across the street from our school, and many kids walk by there. It is dangerous because there is trash and broken glass on the ground.

Underline the opinion, or claim.

Highlight a reason that supports this opinion.

We feel that a community garden would be great in this lot because it would make it look beautiful. It would also help the community since we would be able to grow healthy foods for people. We would like to set up a club to make this happen.

Underline the linking words.

Please help us make our active community more beautiful and safe! Our town needs a community garden on Wells Street.

Highlight the conclusion.

Sincerely,
Gracie Ortez and Dylan Mannion
Mrs. Trigani's Third-Grade Class

Identify Primary and Secondary Sources

A **primary source** is an original document or an account from someone who took part in an event. Your notes and photos from your visit to the park or playground are examples of primary sources.

A **secondary source** is an account from someone who does not have firsthand knowledge of the topic. Secondary sources include textbooks and encyclopedias.

RESEARCH

COLLABORATE Read "Discovering Great Smoky Mountains National Park." Identify some primary and secondary sources in the article. Demonstrate your understanding of the information by explaining how you know which type of source each one is. Discuss with your partner.

Primary Source	How I Know

Secondary Source	How I Know

COLLABORATE Read the two articles and answer the questions.

A Community Garden

by Noah Michaels

On May 1, people gathered for the planting of a community garden. In my interview with the garden's organizer, Cam Ryan, she expressed her thanks for the large community turnout. "I see so many friends and neighbors here willing to lend a hand. It's a great day for our city."

When asked what we would see from the garden later this summer, Ms. Ryan said, "We'll be growing many vegetables, including lettuce, tomatoes, carrots, and potatoes."

Community Garden

A community garden is a large area of land where people can grow flowers, vegetables, and other foods. People gather to plant, tend to the garden, and harvest what they grow. Community gardens can be found in cities where growing space is limited.

1. Which article is an example of a primary source?

_____

2. Which article is an example of a secondary source?

_____

3. What primary source is referenced in one of the articles?

_____

Write a THANK-YOU note

After meeting with the mayor or park official, it is important to thank the person for listening to you or helping with the project. A good way to do this is by writing a thank-you note.

A thank-you note can be structured as follows.

Greeting – Be sure to use the correct title and correct spelling of the name of the person you are addressing.

> Dear Mayor Larkin,

Express your thanks – Begin your note with "Thank you" and state what you are thanking the reader for.

> Thank you for meeting with us.

Add specific details – Add one or more details telling about your cause.

> We hope that you will agree that turning the empty lot into a community garden will help our town.

Give a next step – Write something that you plan to do or that you hope the reader can do to help your cause.

> It's now up to you to approve this lot so it can be used for a beautiful community garden.

Restate your thanks – Thank the person who is reading your letter.

> Thank you again for listening to our idea.

Closing – End your note in a formal way.

> Sincerely,
> Gracie Ortez and Dylan Mannion
> Mrs. Trigani's Third-Grade Class

COLLABORATE With your partner, brainstorm a list of points you want to include in your thank-you note. Look back at your argumentative letter for details about your cause. Then, plan your note. When you have finished, use your plan to write the thank-you note.

THANK YOU!

Greeting

Express your thanks

Add specific details

Give a next step

Restate your thanks

Closing

Revise

Revise by Adding Relevant Details

The writers of the argumentative letter began with a first draft. They read their draft for revision and noticed that some paragraphs needed more details. They wanted to improve the clarity and coherence of the letter, so they added relevant details that directly supported their reasons. They revised some sentences to include additional information.

The vacant lot should be turned into a community
           on Wells Street
garden. The lot is across the street from our school, and
many kids walk by there. It is dangerous.
       because there is trash and broken glass on the ground

Please help us make our community more beautiful!
       active   and safe
Our town needs a community garden on Wells Street.

Reread your draft with your partner. Have you developed a coherent letter by including

☐ reasons to support your opinion?

☐ relevant details to develop an engaging idea?

☐ specific words to focus your reasons?

If needed, go back to your draft and add relevant details.

Edit

Conventions Read your letter again.
Have you used correct writing conventions?

- ☐ spelling
- ☐ punctuation
- ☐ past, present, and future verb tense
- ☐ linking words to connect reasons

Peer Review

COLLABORATE Exchange letters with another group. As you read each letter, try to recognize characteristics of argumentative writing, such as the writer's opinion and the reasons that support the opinion. Then, suggest edits to correct errors in conventions and revisions that could make the letter more convincing.

Presenting in Person

COLLABORATE Imagine your classroom is a town hall and one of your classmates is the mayor or a park official. Present your argumentative letter to the mayor or park official and try to convince him or her to make the improvements discussed in your letter. Remember to use formal language and a confident tone as you address the official. Speak coherently and clearly. After the presentation, allow time for questions and comments. Listen actively, and write some of your classmates' reactions.

_____

_____

_____

Reflect on Your Project

My TURN Think about the argumentative letter you wrote. Which parts of the letter do you think are the strongest? Which areas might you improve next time? Write your thoughts.

Strengths

_____

_____

_____

Areas of Improvement

_____

_____

_____

Reflect on Your Goals

Look back at your unit goals.
Use a different color to rate yourself again.

Reflect on Your Reading

In what ways did the texts you read in this unit relate to your own personal experiences? Synthesize information from the different texts in your answer.

_____

_____

_____

_____

_____

_____

_____

Reflect on Your Writing

What did you like most about writing a personal narrative?

_____

_____

_____

_____

_____

Interactions

Essential Question

How do plants and animals live together?

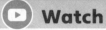 **Watch**

"Living Together"

TURN and TALK

How do plants and animals interact?

SAVVAS
realize™
Go ONLINE for
all lessons.

- ▶ VIDEO
- 🔊 AUDIO
- 👆 INTERACTIVITY
- 🎮 GAME
- ✏ ANNOTATE
- 📖 BOOK
- 🔍 RESEARCH

Spotlight on Informational Text

READING-WRITING BRIDGE

- Academic Vocabulary • Word Study
- **Read Like a Writer • Write for a Reader**
- Spelling • Language and Conventions

WRITING WORKSHOP

- Introduce and Immerse • Develop Elements
- Develop Structure • Writer's Craft
- Publish, Celebrate, and Assess

How-to Article

PROJECT-BASED INQUIRY

- Inquire • Research • Collaborate

Independent Reading

In this unit, you will read informational texts and realistic fiction. If you have a favorite topic, you might choose to read about it during your independent reading time.

To choose an informational text, follow these steps.

Step 1 To help you set a purpose for reading, before you begin, identify what you already know and what you want to learn. New information is easier to remember when you connect it to your background knowledge. Use support from your peers and teachers to read and respond to these prompts.

- I want to read about _____.
- What do I already know about this topic?
- What do I want to learn about this topic?

Step 2 Informational text often presents facts and details about the topic in an organized, structured way. Headings, chapters, and other text features can provide clues to what you will read. Ask yourself questions about the topic as you read. Use the five *W*s and *H*: *Who, What, Where, When, Why,* and *How.* Asking questions will help you find answers.

- What is the topic of the text?
- Why is this topic important?
- How do text features help me understand the topic?

Independent Reading Log

Date	Book	Genre	Pages Read	Minutes Read	My Ratings
					☆☆☆☆☆

Unit Goals

Shade in the circle to rate how well you meet each goal now.

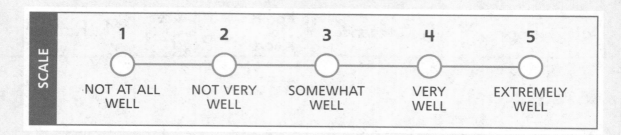

SCALE

1	2	3	4	5
NOT AT ALL WELL	NOT VERY WELL	SOMEWHAT WELL	VERY WELL	EXTREMELY WELL

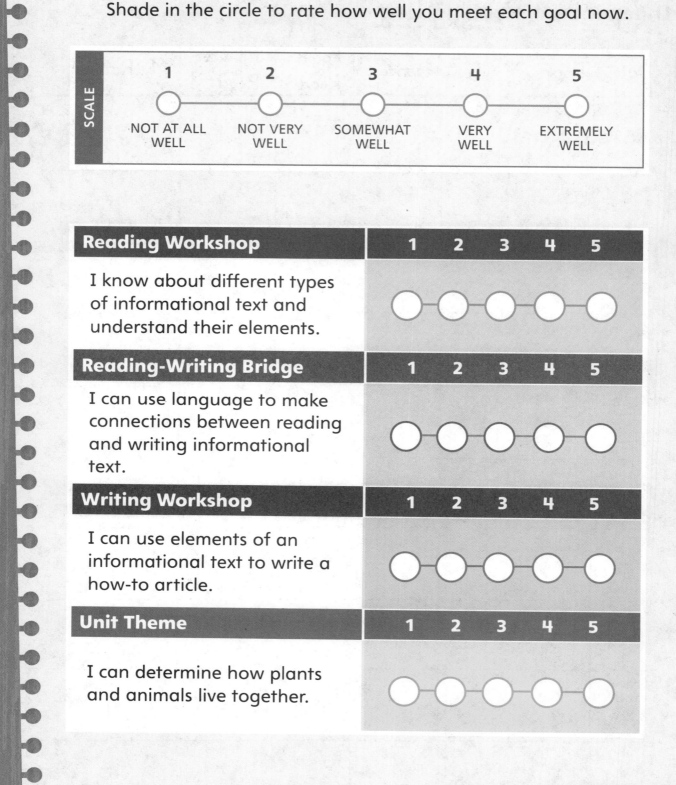

Reading Workshop   1 2 3 4 5

I know about different types of informational text and understand their elements.

Reading-Writing Bridge   1 2 3 4 5

I can use language to make connections between reading and writing informational text.

Writing Workshop   1 2 3 4 5

I can use elements of an informational text to write a how-to article.

Unit Theme   1 2 3 4 5

I can determine how plants and animals live together.

Academic Vocabulary

Use these vocabulary words to talk and write about this unit's theme, *Interactions: associate, prefer, features, investigate,* and *avoid.*

TURN and TALK Read the words and definitions. Then use each word in a sentence. Read your sentences aloud to a partner.

Academic Vocabulary	Definition
associate	to make a connection between two people or things
prefer	to like one thing more than another thing
features	the details or specific traits of something
investigate	to examine or look closely at something
avoid	to stay away from a person, place, or thing

INTERACTIVITY

Amazing Interactions

Animals depend on plants for food, but plants help animals too. Some plants provide camouflage. Camouflage protects animals by hiding them in their environment. Look at each photograph. What do you notice about the animals and the plants around them?

Leopards have spots that blend in with the shadows and sunlight in the trees and grass. This makes it harder for their prey—animals that they eat—to see them.

This **gray tree frog's** skin looks like the tree bark. Other plants growing on the tree also provide camouflage. Gray tree frogs can even change color, depending on their activities or the environment.

Weekly Question

How do patterns in nature help plants and animals?

Turn and Talk Take turns reading aloud sections of the infographic with a partner. Discuss the main ideas and key details. Describe other animals or plants that benefit from camouflage.

This **eastern screech owl's** feathers look like tree bark. These owls are mostly active at night. During the day, they rest in the trees, but they are really hard to see.

A **tiger's** stripes help it blend in with the tall grass in its environment. This plant camouflage helps the tiger sneak up on its prey.

Learning Goal

I can learn more about informational texts and identify the main idea and details in an informational text.

Spotlight on Genre

Informational Text

Informational text is a type of nonfiction text. It usually includes

- One or more **main ideas**
- **Details**, **facts**, and **definitions** that support and explain the main ideas
- **Domain-specific vocabulary** that relates to the topic
- **Features**, such as sections, tables, graphs, time lines, bullets, numbers, and bold and italicized words

You can learn just about anything from informational texts!

TURN and TALK Talk to a partner about an informational text you read recently. What was the main idea? What facts and features supported the information? Take notes on your discussion.

My NOTES

Informational Text Anchor Chart

PURPOSE:

To explain or inform readers about a topic

Types of Informational Texts

- **Biography:** an author's retelling of factual events in a person's life

- **Autobiography:** a retelling of factual events in one's own life

- **Steps in a process:** a detailed explanation of a process

- **Social studies, science, history, and art books:** nonfiction books that teach a particular subject

Jennifer Roy and **Gregory Roy** have co-authored several informational books about math. Some of the titles include *Holiday Fractions*, *Measuring at Home*, and *Graphing in the Desert*. Jennifer is also an award-winning children's novelist. She wrote a series about twin sisters with her real-life twin sister, Julia.

Patterns in Nature

Preview Vocabulary

As you read *Patterns in Nature*, notice these words and how they help you identify the main idea and details.

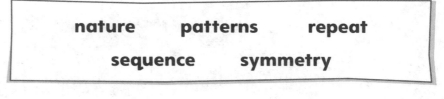

nature	patterns	repeat
sequence	symmetry	

Read

Asking questions before reading helps deepen your understanding of a text. To do this, skim the text and ask questions about what you will learn. Follow these strategies when you read this text the first time.

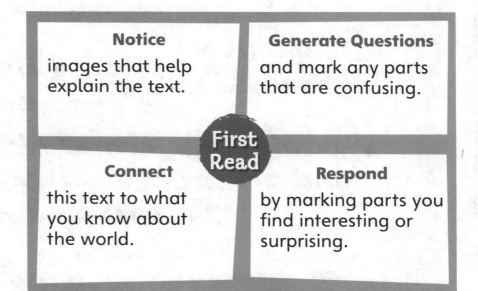

Notice images that help explain the text.

Generate Questions and mark any parts that are confusing.

First Read

Connect this text to what you know about the world.

Respond by marking parts you find interesting or surprising.

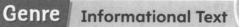

Patterns in Nature

by Jennifer Rozines Roy and Gregory Roy

🔊 AUDIO

✏️ ANNOTATE

Identify Main Idea and Details

<u>Underline</u> the details that tell you how to identify a pattern.

nature the things around us not made by humans

patterns sets of things that repeat in order

1   Step outside. Nature is all around you. Plants, birds, animals, and insects make the world their home. Look closely, and you'll notice something cool—patterns!

2   A pattern is a set of things that are repeated again and again in a certain order. Patterns can be made with shapes, lines, and numbers.

3   It's a beautiful day for a nature walk. Grab a jacket and let's discover more about patterns!

4   Our search begins in the backyard. First you'll see a tall tree. It is covered with green leaves.

5   There is no special order to the leaves. They do not form any pattern.

CLOSE READ

Monitor Comprehension

Reread paragraphs 4 and 5. Highlight evidence that describes two key details about leaf patterns.

Identify Main Idea and Details

Underline an example of a repeating pattern. How does this example help you recognize the main idea of the text?

repeat to happen over and over

6   Pick up one twig from the ground and pick one leaf from the tree. Lay them down side by side. Place another twig and another leaf next to them in a line.

7   *Twig, leaf, twig, leaf.* We're making a pattern!

8   Keep putting down more twigs and leaves, following the pattern. This is called a repeating pattern. The objects repeat themselves over and over.

9 Rows of tasty vegetables grow in the garden. Some of the vegetables form patterns.

10 The different sizes make up this pattern. The patten rule is *large, small.*

11 A pattern rule describes how things are arranged. This row of colorful peppers is a pattern, too. The pattern rule is *red, green, green, yellow.*

Monitor Comprehension

Highlight a detail that tells you what a pattern rule is. Use your background knowledge, or what you already know, about patterns to help you understand this detail.

Vocabulary in Context

Context clues are words and sentences around an unfamiliar word that help readers understand the word.

Use a context clue beyond the sentence to determine the meaning of *colorful.*

Underline the context clue that supports your definition.

12 Patterns can be made from different numbers of objects. We can create patterns using sets of green beans. Let's use the pattern rule *4, 3, 1*.

13 Drop the beans in this basket to save for later. There's no pattern in the beans now!

14 Look! A ladybug is sitting on this flower.

Identify Main Idea and Details

Underline supporting details about a growing number sequence.

sequence a series of things in order

15   Here is a pattern of ladybugs.

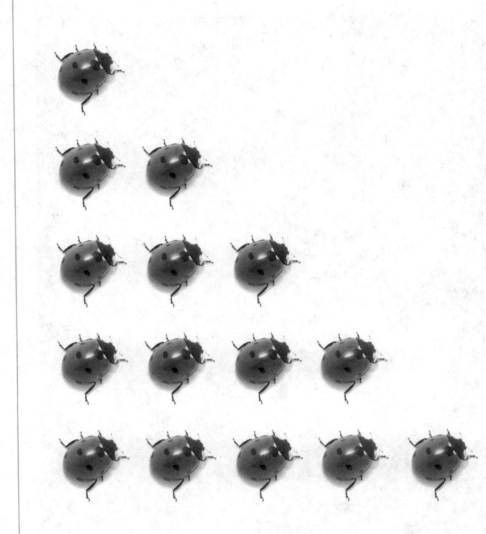

16   The pattern rule is *1, 2, 3, 4, 5.* This is called a growing number sequence. A sequence is a series of numbers in order. This sequence "grows" from small to large.

17   Each ladybug has two wings. The pattern rule for the ladybugs' wings is *2, 4, 6, 8, 10*. It's also a growing number sequence.

CLOSE READ

Monitor Comprehension

Look at the picture of the ladybugs. Highlight the pattern rule in the text that describes what the picture shows.

18   This ladybug is spreading her wings. Ladybug, ladybug, fly away!

Identify Main Idea and Details

Underline the details that describe the pattern rule of color. How do these details help you recognize the main idea?

19 There are lots of rocks in the backyard. Let's make a pattern of different color stones. *White, gray, white, black* is the pattern rule here.

Monitor Comprehension

Reread paragraph 20. Highlight details that describe a different pattern rule for the rocks.

20 Now let's make a number sequence that counts by *3: 3, 6, 9, 12, 15.* That rocks!

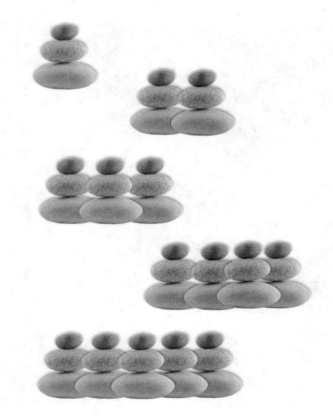

21   Good thing you're wearing a jacket. It's starting to rain. But up in the sky is a rainbow!

22   The colors on a rainbow are always in the same order: red, orange, yellow, green, blue, indigo, violet.

23   A rainbow is a pattern of colors across the sky!

CLOSE READ

Monitor Comprehension

Highlight details you could reread to help you understand the way the pattern rule of a rainbow is determined.

Identify Main Idea and Details

<u>Underline</u> details that explain a repeating pattern in nature. How do these details help you recognize the main idea?

24   Did you know nature follows a pattern? The seasons repeat themselves year after year in the same order: *spring, summer, fall, winter, spring, summer, fall, winter.*

25   Nature looks different as each season passes.

26   In springtime, many creatures come out from their winter homes. This butterfly was tucked in a cocoon, but now it's out.

27   The butterfly is symmetrical. Its left wing has the same spotted pattern as the right wing.

28   When a pattern is the same on both sides of an object, the object has **symmetry**.

CLOSE READ

Identify Main Idea and Details

<u>Underline</u> details that explain a butterfly's special pattern.

symmetry being the same on both sides

Look at the pictures of snowflakes. Highlight a detail in the text that helps you understand what you see in the pictures about symmetry.

29   Other things in nature have symmetry. Snowflakes have the same pattern on both sides.

30   And this leaf has symmetry, too.

31   Patterns are all around us. They make nature beautiful and they help us make sense of our world.

32   What patterns do *you* see in nature?

CLOSE READ

Identify Main Idea and Details

Underline the details about the effect that patterns have on the world. Explain how these details help you recognize the main idea.

Develop Vocabulary

Authors often use domain-specific words, or words that relate to the topic, in informational text. Domain-specific words can help readers better understand the main ideas and details in the text.

My TURN Draw a line from each word to its definition. Then complete the sentences.

a series of things in order	being the same on both sides	sets of things that repeat in order

patterns   sequence   symmetry

1. Patterns in nature include _____

_____ .

2. An example of a **sequence** is _____

_____ .

3. An example of **symmetry** in nature is _____

_____

Check for Understanding

My TURN Look back at the text to answer the questions.

1. How do you know that *Patterns in Nature* is informational text?

2. Why do the authors compare a butterfly's wings to a snowflake in paragraphs 27–29?

3. By the end of the text, what can the reader conclude about pattern rules?

4. How are a sequence and a pattern related? Cite text evidence in your analysis.

Identify Main Idea and Details

The **main idea** is the most important idea about a topic. **Details** are facts, examples, and other information about the topic. They support the main idea. As you read, evaluate details to help you determine the main idea. Explain how the details support the main idea.

1. **My TURN** Go to the Close Read notes in *Patterns in Nature* and underline the parts that help you identify the main idea and details.

2. **Text Evidence** Use some of the evidence you underlined to complete the chart. Identify key details in the text and evaluate the details to determine the main idea.

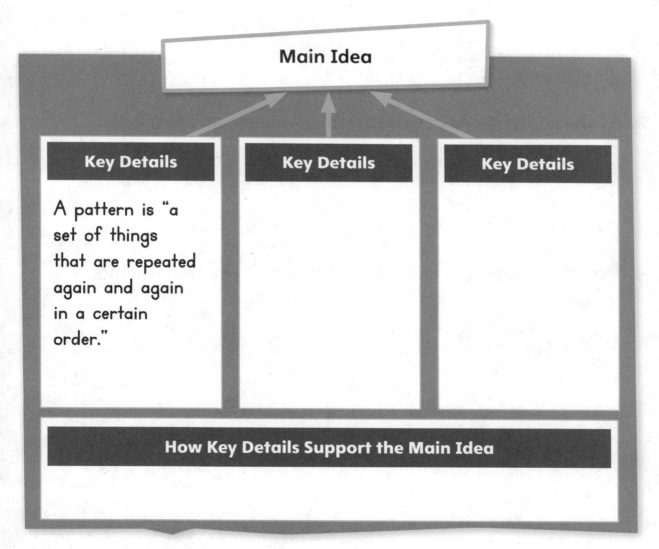

Main Idea

Key Details

A pattern is "a set of things that are repeated again and again in a certain order."

Key Details

Key Details

How Key Details Support the Main Idea

Monitor Comprehension

As you read, monitor your understanding of the main idea and details. Notice whether the text makes sense to you. Use strategies to help you understand the text, such as rereading, using background knowledge, asking questions, and annotating the text.

1. **My TURN** Go back to the Close Read notes and highlight evidence that helps you understand the main idea and details.

2. **Text Evidence** Use some of your highlighted text to monitor your comprehension of the text.

Text I Did Not Understand	Comprehension Strategy I Used	How the Strategy Helped
"There is no special order to the leaves. They do not form any pattern."	I reread the text about what a pattern is and looked at the photo.	I understood that leaves do not form a set that repeats in a certain order.

Reflect and Share

Talk About It The authors of *Patterns in Nature* describe some of the patterns that occur in plants, animals, the sky, and the seasons. What other patterns have you read about in texts this week? What patterns in nature have you seen? Use text evidence to discuss how patterns help plants and animals survive.

Ask Relevant Questions When listening, it is important to ask relevant questions about ideas you do not understand.

◎ Do not interrupt the speaker. Raise your hand and wait to be called on.

◎ Make your questions clear and related to the topic.

◎ Listen carefully to all speakers.

Use these sentence starters to guide your questions:

I do not understand how . . .

Please explain why . . .

Weekly Question

How do patterns in nature help plants and animals?

Academic Vocabulary

Related Words share roots or word parts. They can have different meanings based on how the word is used, such as *explore*, *explorer*, and *exploration*.

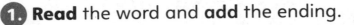

Learning Goal

I can develop knowledge about language to make connections between reading and writing.

My TURN For each sentence below,

1. **Read** the word and **add** the ending.

2. **Use** a print or digital dictionary to find the meaning and spelling of the related word.

3. **Write** a sentence using the new word.

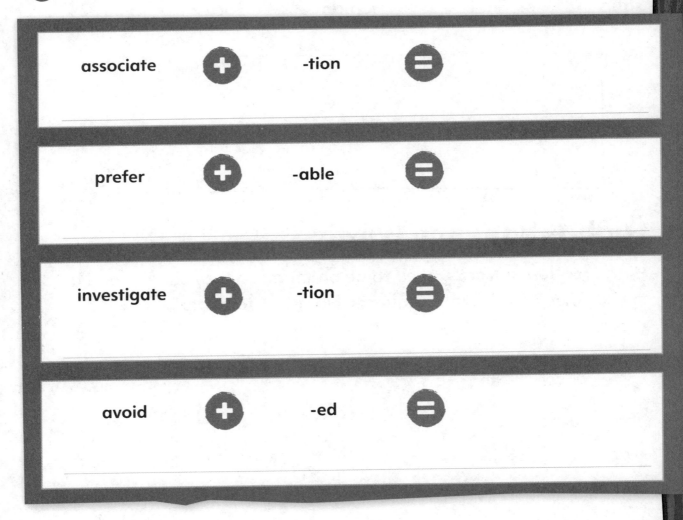

associate   **+**   -tion   **=**

_____

prefer   **+**   -able   **=**

_____

investigate   **+**   -tion   **=**

_____

avoid   **+**   -ed   **=**

_____

Syllable Patterns

Syllable Patterns VC/V and V/CV Two-syllable words that have one consonant in the middle may have the VC/V or V/CV pattern.

Look at the word *nature* in paragraph 1 of *Patterns in Nature*. It has the V/CV pattern: *na / ture*. The first syllable ends in a vowel which spells a long *a* sound. It is an open syllable. The first syllable in the word *finish* ends in a consonant. It has the VC/V pattern: *fin / ish*. Syllables that end in consonant sounds are closed syllables.

My TURN Read each word. Then sort the words by their syllable pattern.

tiger	wagon	lizard	paper
satin	final	lemon	focus

VC/V	V/CV

High-Frequency Words

High-frequency words need to be practiced so they can be read quickly in texts. Read these high-frequency words: *certain*, *half*.

Read Like a Writer

Authors use graphic features in informational texts to help readers understand ideas. In *Patterns in Nature*, the authors use illustrations to show information about patterns.

Model ! Look at the image from *Patterns in Nature*.

visual information

1. Identify The pattern rule is *red, green, green, yellow*.

2. Question How does the image help me see a pattern rule?

3. Conclude I can use color to see a pattern rule.

Look at the image.

My TURN Follow the steps to analyze the image.

1. Identify The pattern rule is _____ .

2. Question How does the image help me see a pattern rule?

3. Conclude I can use _____ to see a pattern rule.

Write for a Reader

When you read informational text, look for graphic features such as illustrations to help you understand ideas or concepts in the text.

Think of interesting ways to illustrate your ideas!

My TURN Think about how Jennifer Roy and Gregory Roy used images to show different concepts about patterns in *Patterns in Nature*. Identify a pattern you learned about. Write about the pattern and use an illustration to show the pattern.

1. Write a sentence that tells about a pattern.

_____

_____

2. Draw an illustration that shows the pattern.

3. Explain how your illustration shows the details that you described in your sentence.

_____

_____

Spell Syllable Patterns

Syllable patterns VC/V and V/CV can be used to help you remember how to spell words. Divide a VC/V word after the consonant. Divide a V/CV word before the consonant. A print or digital dictionary can help you divide words into syllables.

My TURN Sort the words by their syllable patterns. Use a print or digital dictionary to check your syllabication.

SPELLING WORDS

total	minus	equal
digit	defend	salad
talent	finish	famous
human		

VC/V

_____

_____

_____

_____

V/CV

_____

_____

_____

_____

_____

High-Frequency Words

High-frequency words appear often in texts. Read these high-frequency words and write them on the lines.

certain _____

half _____

Singular and Plural Nouns

Singular nouns name one person, place, or thing. **Plural nouns** name more than one. For most nouns, add -s or -es to form plurals. For nouns that end with a consonant + *y*, change *y* to *i* and add -es. Some **irregular plural nouns** are not formed in a usual way. Sometimes the singular and plural forms are the same.

Rule	Singular	Plural
add -s	dog, room, tree, computer, chair	dogs, rooms, trees, computers, chairs
add -es to words that end in *sh*, *ch*, *tch*, *x*, *s*, or *ss*	ash, inch, watch, fox, circus, glass	ashes, inches, watches, foxes, circuses, glasses
consonant + *y*, change *y* to *i* and add -es	lady, copy, hobby	ladies, copies, hobbies
irregular plurals	man, mouse, deer	men, mice, deer

My TURN Edit this draft by correcting errors in singular and plural nouns. Spell each word correctly.

> A women walked her two dog down the trail. In the
> woods, she saw fox running. Later, she heard a group
> of deers as their hoof made crunching noises on all the
> fallen leaf.

How-to Article

How-to articles explain a process or how to do something, such as flying a kite or making a pizza.

My TURN Select a how-to article from the classroom library. Then complete the chart.

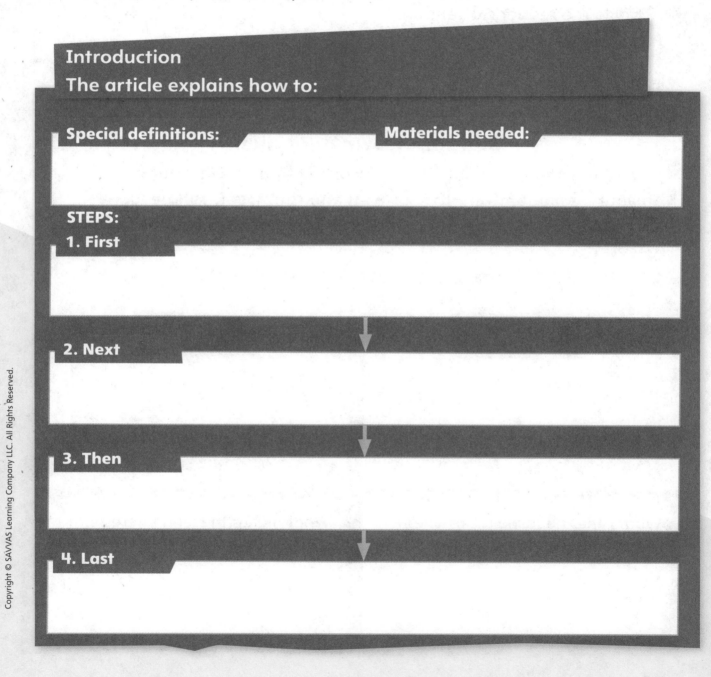

Introduction
The article explains how to:

Special definitions: **Materials needed:**

STEPS:

1. First

2. Next

3. Then

4. Last

Compose a Headline and Lead

A how-to article has a **headline** instead of a title. The **lead** is similar to an introduction. The lead is brief, interesting, and to the point.

A good lead

- Informs the reader of the topic
- Attracts the reader's attention
- Includes a clear main idea

My TURN Read the passage. Then complete the chart. Share your ideas.

Start Your Own Aquarium

Imagine graceful goldfish and colorful guppies swimming in your own aquarium. To set up an aquarium, you will need equipment, a few fish, and, of course, fish food. Are you ready to get started?

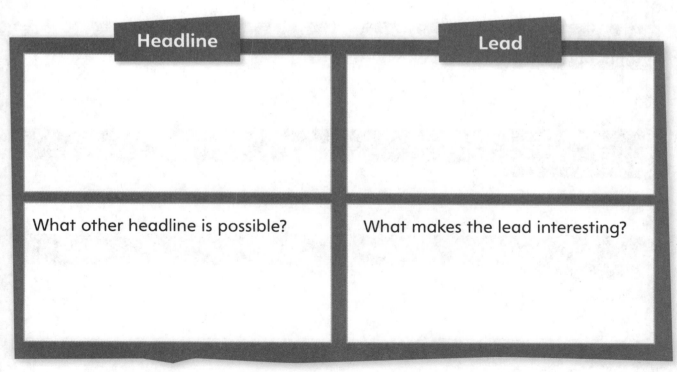

Headline	Lead
What other headline is possible?	What makes the lead interesting?

Compose Facts and Details

A how-to article includes **facts**. A fact is a statement that can be proved. **Details** are also used in informational texts. Details support the facts.

Fact: Some gardens include herbs. **Details:** The herb rosemary is easy to grow. It has beautiful green leaves and small blue flowers. Rosemary smells great and tastes wonderful in food.

My TURN Read a how-to article from your classroom library. Work with a partner to complete the chart. Find and list three facts. Then list details that support each fact.

Fact 1	Fact 2	Fact 3
Details	**Details**	**Details**

Brainstorm and Set a Purpose

When writers brainstorm, they are open to all ideas. As you brainstorm ideas for your how-to article, think about your purpose. Once you have your list of topics, focus on who will read your article. Knowing your audience will help you plan your explanation.

My **TURN** Develop a list of possible topics for a how-to article. Then identify the purpose and audience for your how-to article.

Topics can include things you do well. What are some things you do well and could explain to others?

_____

_____

The **purpose** of a how-to article is to explain a process. What process do you want to explain?

_____

The **audience** needs to understand the steps you explain. Who will most likely read your how-to article?

_____

As you brainstorm for your how-to article, use this checklist to help you focus your steps.

WRITE FOR YOUR AUDIENCE

☐ I will list the important steps of the process.

☐ I will list the steps in order.

☐ I will make my instructions clear and simple.

Plan Your How-to Article

To gather ideas for a how-to article, writers might brainstorm, freewrite, or map. A writer who freewrites records ideas quickly without stopping.

My TURN Freewrite about the steps in your process on a separate sheet of paper. Then map the steps in the chart. Share your ideas with your Writing Club. Listen to others. Ask and answer questions about the organization. Exchange comments until the steps are in the best order.

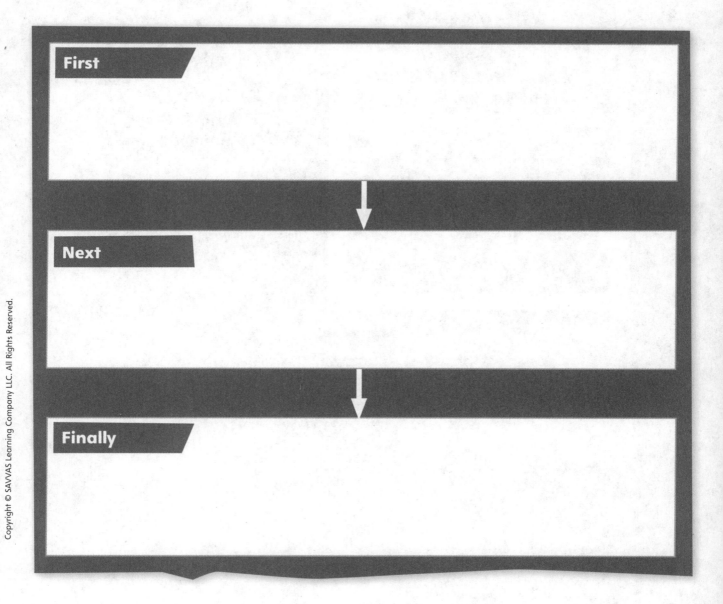

First

Next

Finally

 INTERACTIVITY

On the AFRICAN SAVANNA

The savanna is an enormous grassland in Africa. The weather is warm and there is plenty of sunshine.

AFRICA

Savanna

 Watch

The savanna is home to a variety of animals and plants, such as termites, lions, and trees. Watch the video clip to learn more about life on the savanna.

Some animals on the savanna, such as zebras and antelope, are called **herbivores** because they eat only plants. Other animals, such as lions and cheetahs, are **predators**. They kill and eat **prey**, such as zebras and antelope.

AFRICAN SAVANNA about 5.2 million square miles

UNITED STATES about 3.8 million square miles

Termites and other insects on the savanna eat dead trees. These animals are called **decomposers**. When a dead tree decomposes, or breaks down, it becomes rich soil that helps new trees grow. Decomposers help the regrowth of plants on the savanna.

Weekly Question

How do living things in a habitat support one another?

Turn and Talk Read these pages. Then watch and talk about the video with a partner. Discuss what the multimedia texts tell you about life on the savanna and how living things interact. Speak clearly and talk at a rate and volume appropriate for a discussion. Take notes on your discussion.

Spotlight on Genre

Informational Text

Text structure is the way a piece of writing is organized. Writers of informational text choose the text structure that best helps readers understand the information. Some common text structures include

- Sequence
- Cause and effect
- Problem and solution

Establish Purpose The **purpose**, or reason, for reading an informational text is often to learn more about a particular topic.

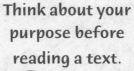

Think about your purpose before reading a text.

My **PURPOSE**

_____

_____

_____

_____

TURN and TALK With a partner, discuss different purposes for reading *Weird Friends*. Then set your purpose for reading this text.

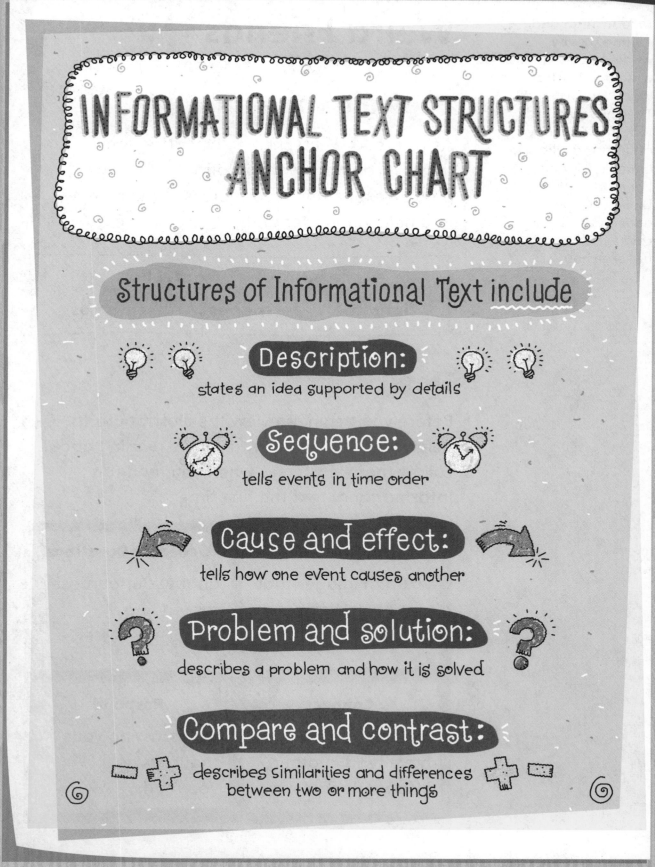

INFORMATIONAL TEXT STRUCTURES ANCHOR CHART

Structures of Informational Text include

Description:
states an idea supported by details

Sequence:
tells events in time order

Cause and effect:
tells how one event causes another

Problem and solution:
describes a problem and how it is solved

Compare and contrast:
describes similarities and differences
between two or more things

Meet the Author

Jose Aruego and **Ariane Dewey** worked as a team to write and illustrate *Weird Friends*. They have worked together on many other books about animals, including *We Hide, You Seek*. Dewey, a painter, added her vibrant colors to Aruego's fun sketches.

Weird Friends

Preview Vocabulary

As you read *Weird Friends*, pay attention to these vocabulary words. Notice how they provide explanations for details in the text and help you better understand the topic.

predators	**protection**
immune	**species** **emerges**

Read

Before you begin, preview the illustrations to help you picture what you will be reading about. Follow these strategies when you read this **informational text** the first time.

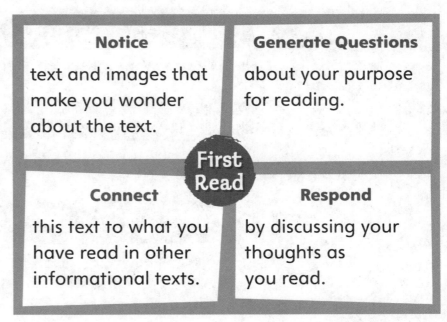

Notice text and images that make you wonder about the text.

Generate Questions about your purpose for reading.

First Read

Connect this text to what you have read in other informational texts.

Respond by discussing your thoughts as you read.

Weird Friends

Unlikely Allies in the Animal Kingdom

by Jose Aruego and Ariane Dewey

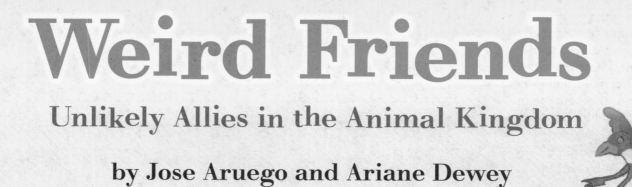

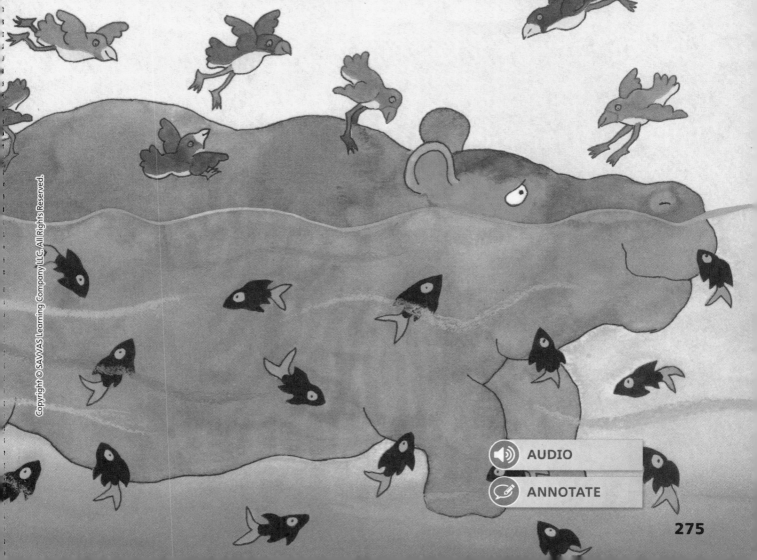

AUDIO

ANNOTATE

Evaluate Details

Highlight the series of details that describes different ways that animals help one another to survive. Evaluate these details to determine an important idea.

predators animals that live by eating other animals

protection safety

1   Sometimes in the wild, animals you might think could hurt each other actually help each other in surprising ways. They share food or a home. They warn one another of approaching predators. They cluster side by side for protection. Some animals even give others a good bath. Their survival often depends on these weird friendships.

The Clown Fish and the Sea Anemone

2   The bright little clown fish needs protection from its enemies. So it chooses a poisonous sea anemone to be its bodyguard. For about an hour, the clown fish carefully darts in and out of the anemone's deadly tentacles. Little by little, it becomes immune to their sting. Then it moves in. The clown fish is safe from predators. So is the anemone, because its enemy, the butterfly fish, is afraid of the clown fish's bite.

CLOSE READ

Analyze Text Structure

Underline the details that help you recognize the clown fish's problem and the solution to its problem.

immune not affected by something, such as an illness

Vocabulary in Context

Context clues are words and sentences around an unfamiliar word that help readers understand the word.

Use context clues before and within the sentence to determine the meaning of *attention*.

Underline the context clue that supports your definition.

The Rhino and the Cattle Egret

3   As they graze across the plains, a rhino and her calf stir up grasshoppers. But the rhino can't see very well and may not notice danger approaching. So she lets a sharp-eyed cattle egret perch on her back to act as a lookout. The egret is rewarded with an endless feast of grasshoppers.

4   If the egret spies danger, it screams. And if *that* doesn't get the rhino's attention, it taps on the rhino's head until the mother and baby gallop to safety.

The Blind Shrimp and the Goby

5 One species of shrimp is completely blind. But it knows how to get help. It digs a hole in the sand, crawls in, and waits for a goby fish to swim in for shelter. The goby has a place to hide, and the blind shrimp has a guide to lead it when it's safe to go out.

6 While they're feeding, the shrimp's antennae feel the goby's every move. If a predator approaches, the goby flicks its tail, and the two swim quickly back into their safe burrow.

CLOSE READ

Analyze Text Structure

<u>Underline</u> details in paragraph 5 that allow you to recognize the shrimp's problem and the solution to its problem.

species a group of living things that are the same in most ways

The Ostrich and the Zebra

Evaluate Details

Highlight details about ostriches and zebras that explain the advantages they have against predators. How do these details help you understand how animals can protect each other?

7   Ostriches have terrific eyes. Zebras have terrific ears. When the two get together, nothing can sneak up on them. That's why ostriches and zebras often roam the savanna together, chomping on seeds and grasses.

8   The ostriches look, and the zebras listen, for predators. The first to detect a hungry lion warns the others, and before it can attack, they all flee to safety.

The Red Phalaropes and the Sperm Whale

9   The red phalaropes follow a pod of sperm whales as they swim far out to sea. The birds hover over the water and wait for a whale to come up for air.

10   As soon as a whale surfaces, the birds land on its back and begin to pry parasites from cuts and cracks in its skin. Being free of these pests makes the whale feel better, and the phalaropes enjoy a tasty meal. But the birds have to eat quickly, because once the whale blows, it takes a breath, slaps its tail, and dives deep into the ocean.

Analyze Text Structure

<u>Underline</u> words and phrases that show the sequence of the ants' activities. Explain how this text structure contributes to the author's purpose.

emerges to come out of a hidden place

The Red Ants and the Large Blue Butterfly

11   When red ants find a particular type of caterpillar, they lug it back to their nest. There, they tickle its tummy till it oozes the sweet honeydew they love to sip. In return, the ants feed the caterpillar all it can eat. The caterpillar lives unharmed in the ants' nest for eleven months, eating and pupating. Finally, it emerges as a Large Blue Butterfly, shakes out its wings, and flies away. Soon, the ants will go in search of another caterpillar.

The Hermit Crab and the Sea Anemones

12   When a hermit crab needs a new home, it finds an empty shell, moves in, and sticks sea anemones on top for protection. The anemones' stinging tentacles scare away octopuses, which love to eat hermit crabs. Anemones can't walk, so the crab provides them with transportation to new feeding spots. And because crabs are messy eaters, there are always food scraps for the anemones to nibble.

CLOSE READ

Vocabulary in Context

Use a context clue within the sentence to determine the meaning of *transportation*.

Underline the context clue that supports your definition.

The Impalas and the Baboons

13 At the water hole, a herd of delicate impalas stays close to a troop of tough baboons. The impalas use their excellent senses of smell, hearing, and sight to detect danger.

14 If the impalas notice a predator approaching, they dance nervously. That warns the baboons, who bare their fangs and snarl to scare the attacker away.

The Horse Mackerel and the Portuguese Man-of-War

15 When the horse mackerel is pursued by an enemy, it races for home.

16 The mackerel's home is a colony of small organisms living together called a Portuguese man-of-war. It has venomous ribbons that can reach seventy feet long and that shoot paralyzing, barbed harpoons into whatever they touch. But they don't harm the horse mackerel, because it doesn't feel their sting. The mackerel is safe and the man-of-war is well fed, because any predator that comes too close will end up as the man-of-war's dinner.

CLOSE READ

Evaluate Details

Highlight information about the man-of-war and horse mackerel. Evaluate the details in the text to determine an important idea.

Evaluate Details

Highlight phrases that tell how the forest mouse and hippo are helped by other animals.

The Forest Mouse and the Beetles

17 At night, the forest mouse scampers around the rain forest looking for food, with beetles clinging to its fur and face. But the mouse doesn't mind, because the beetles eat the fleas that infest its fur. During the day, while the mouse sleeps, the beetles dismount and eat the bugs in the mouse's burrow. The beetles are always well fed, and the mouse and its house are free of itchy insects.

The Hippo, the Oxpeckers, and the Black Labeo Fish

18 The hippo can't scrub itself, so it wades into the river and waits for oxpeckers to land on its back. These birds peck off and eat ticks and other bothersome bugs. Meanwhile, in the water below, black labeo fish gobble up anything clinging to the rest of the hippo. When all the parasites have been removed, the hippo naps in the cool mud.

The Wrasse and the Google-Eye Fish

19   When the wrasse is hungry, it dances on its head and wags its tail to announce that its cleaning station is open. Soon, lots of filthy google-eye fish are lining up for a bath. Like a small vacuum with teeth, the wrasse nips gunk from gills and scours parasites off scales. All the fish get a good washing, and the wrasse has a hearty meal.

CLOSE READ

Analyze Text Structure

Underline details that help you recognize the cause and effect of the wrasse opening its cleaning station.

Evaluate Details

Highlight details that explain why the sooty shearwater allows the tuatara to stay in its burrow.

The Tuatara and the Sooty Shearwater

20   The tuatara is a slow and lazy reptile. It rarely even builds its own nest. Instead, the tuatara finds a sooty shearwater's cliff-top burrow and moves in while the bird is out.

21   But the tuatara is a good guest. It licks up every last slug, moth, worm, and beetle in the tunnel. When the sooty shearwater returns, the nest is clean, and the tuatara is welcome to stay.

The Water Thick-Knees and the Crocodile

22   A bird called a water thick-knees sometimes builds its nest next to a crocodile's home. When the crocodile leaves to go hunting, the bird watches both of their nests.

23   If trouble threatens the eggs or young in either nest, the bird screeches until the crocodile comes charging home. The water thick-knees and her family are safe beside their ferocious neighbor, because the crocodile will not eat its babysitter.

CLOSE READ

Analyze Text Structure

Underline the effects of water thick-knees building their nests near crocodile nests.

Develop Vocabulary

In informational text, authors often use specific words that explain the topic. When reading informational texts about nature, notice scientific words that describe living things and how they behave.

My TURN Add the vocabulary word from the word bank to tell what the author is describing. Then complete the remaining columns of the chart.

Word Bank

immune   species   predators

Vocabulary Word	The author is describing . . .	This word helps me know . . .	Example Sentence
	animals that live by eating other animals.		
	a group of living things that are the same in most ways.		
	a living thing unaffected by something, such as an illness.		

Check for Understanding

My TURN Look back at the text to answer the questions.

1. How can the reader identify *Weird Friends* as informational text?

2. Why do you think the authors included headings and sections in the text?

3. What can the reader conclude about the relationship between zebras and ostriches?

4. How would you prove that a pair of animal friends can help each other survive? Use text evidence in your response.

Analyze Text Structure

Authors use **text structure** to organize information. Recognizing text structure helps readers understand ideas and how ideas are related. One type of text structure shows problems and solutions.

1. **MyTURN** Go to the Close Read notes in *Weird Friends*. Underline the parts that help you analyze text structure.

2. **Text Evidence** Use some of the parts you underlined to complete the chart.

Animal	Problem	Solution
clown fish	"The bright little clown fish needs protection from its enemies."	"So it chooses a poisonous sea anemone to be its bodyguard."
blind shrimp		

How does the problem-and-solution text structure help you understand the text?

Evaluate Details

While reading informational text, look for **details** that help you understand important ideas. Evaluate, or judge, which details best support these ideas.

1. **My TURN** Go back to the Close Read notes and highlight details that help you understand important ideas.

2. **Text Evidence** Use your highlighted text to evaluate details. Cite the details that help you determine important ideas.

Animal Friends	Details	Important Ideas
ostrich and zebra	"The ostriches look, and the zebras listen, for predators."	Animals can warn each other of danger.
horse mackerel and Portuguese man-of-war		
forest mouse and beetles		

Reflect and Share

Write to Sources In this unit so far, you have read about patterns in nature and animal friendships. How do patterns and helping relationships help plants and animals survive? Use evidence from the texts to write a response to this question.

Respond to Informational Text When you respond to informational text, you consider the facts and details presented before you begin writing. Narrow your focus by asking yourself questions:

◎ What is my purpose for writing?

◎ What details from the text are relevant to my response?

◎ How will my response show an understanding of the information in the text?

Write one sentence that responds to the prompt. Identify details from the texts that tell about the survival of plants and animals. Use those details to support your response. Write your response on a separate sheet of paper.

Weekly Question

How do living things in a habitat support one another?

Academic Vocabulary

Synonyms and Antonyms Words that have the same or similar meanings are **synonyms**. For example, *cold* and *frigid* are synonyms. Words that have opposite meanings are **antonyms**. *Hot* and *cold* are antonyms. Finding synonyms and antonyms can deepen your understanding of a word's meaning.

My TURN For each word below,

1. **Read** the definition of each word.

2. **Write** a synonym and explain its meaning.

3. **Write** an antonym and explain its meaning.

4. **Use** a print or digital dictionary or thesaurus as needed.

Synonyms	Words	Antonyms
connect	**associate:** to make a connection between two people or things	disassociate, disconnect
	prefer: to like something more than another thing	
	investigate: to examine or look closely at something	
	avoid: to keep away from a person, place, or thing	

r-Controlled Vowels

r-Controlled Vowels are vowels that are followed by the letter *r*. The *r* changes the sound of the vowel. The *r*-controlled vowel sound you hear in the word *part* can be spelled *ar*. The *r*-controlled vowel sound you hear in the word *port* can be spelled *or*, *ore*, or *oar*.

My TURN Read each word with an *r*-controlled vowel. Then write each word in the correct column based on how the sound is spelled.

before	garden	onboard
forest	hardy	organisms

Sound of *ar*	Sound of *or*		
ar	or	ore	oar

High-Frequency Words

High-frequency words are words that you will see many times as you read. Read these high-frequency words: *finally*, *money*.

Read Like a Writer

Authors use literal language, such as precise verbs, to convey a specific meaning.

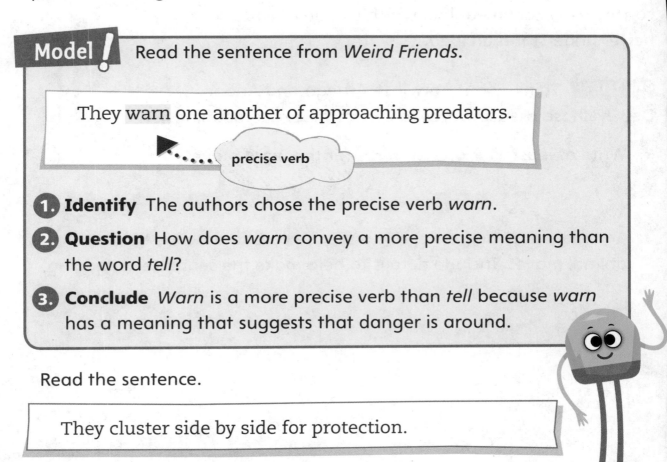

Model !   Read the sentence from *Weird Friends.*

> They **warn** one another of approaching predators.
>
> ◀ ·····• precise verb

1. **Identify** The authors chose the precise verb *warn*.

2. **Question** How does *warn* convey a more precise meaning than the word *tell*?

3. **Conclude** *Warn* is a more precise verb than *tell* because *warn* has a meaning that suggests that danger is around.

Read the sentence.

> They cluster side by side for protection.

My TURN Follow the steps to analyze the sentence. Describe how the authors use a precise verb.

1. **Identify** The authors chose the precise verb _____.

2. **Question** How does the verb convey a more precise meaning than the word *stand*?

3. **Conclude** The verb _____ is a more precise verb than *stand* because _____

_____.

Write for a Reader

You can use a thesaurus to find a precise verb.

Writers use precise verbs to make their writing more accurate and engaging. A precise verb conveys an exact meaning, which can help readers better understand an idea.

My TURN Think about how Jose Aruego and Ariane Dewey chose precise words to convey an exact meaning.

1. Write at least four precise verbs for the word *move*.

_____

2. Complete each sentence. Use a precise verb to describe how the animal moves. Include details to help make the sentences engaging.

The dog _____

_____ .

The snake _____

_____ .

The clown fish _____

_____ .

The rhino _____

_____ .

3. On a separate sheet of paper, describe how the verbs you chose help you achieve the purpose of telling exactly how the animals move.

Spell Words with *r*-Controlled Vowels

Words with *r*-Controlled Vowels When a vowel is followed by the letter *r*, the *r* changes the sound of the vowel. The *r*-controlled vowel sound you hear in the word **part** can be spelled **ar**. The *r*-controlled vowel sound you hear in the word **port** can be spelled **or**, **ore**, or **oar**.

SPELLING WORDS		
morning	soared	adore
format	darkness	target
explore	alarm	absorb
cardboard		

My TURN Sort words by their spelling patterns.

oar
_____

_____

ar
_____

_____

_____

ore
_____

_____

or
_____

_____

_____

High-Frequency Words

Read these high-frequency words and write them on the lines.

finally _____

money _____

Irregular Plural Nouns

Irregular Plural Nouns are not formed in usual ways. You will need to memorize irregular plurals in order to use them correctly.

Singular Noun	Irregular Plural Noun
man	men
woman	women
child	children
mouse	mice
deer	deer
sheep	sheep
fish	fish (or fishes)

Singular Noun	Irregular Plural Noun
foot	feet
tooth	teeth
goose	geese
leaf	leaves
life	lives
ox	oxen
moose	moose

My TURN Edit this draft by replacing the incorrect singular nouns with the correct irregular plural nouns.

Two man and two child watched the deer run through the meadow. A flock of goose flew overhead as the weather turned cold. By the barn, the group of sheep huddled to stay out of the wind. Several mouse scurried to make nests. The leaf blew off the trees. Winter was on its way.

Develop an Engaging Main Idea

Writers structure their writing to develop an engaging main idea that excites readers. If a how-to article is not engaging, readers may not finish it.

My TURN　Review three how-to articles from your classroom library. Identify each book's main idea and what makes it engaging for readers.

Book Title:

Main Idea:
Why Is It Engaging?

Book Title:

Main Idea:
Why Is It Engaging?

Book Title:

Main Idea:
Why Is It Engaging?

My TURN　In your writing notebook, begin to compose a structured draft of your how-to article by developing an engaging main idea.

Develop Relevant Details

Relevant details keep a how-to article focused on the main idea. Relevant details also give organization, or structure, to a how-to article. To choose relevant details, writers select only the details that are related to the topic.

My TURN Write your engaging main idea in the top box. Then develop it by writing relevant details.

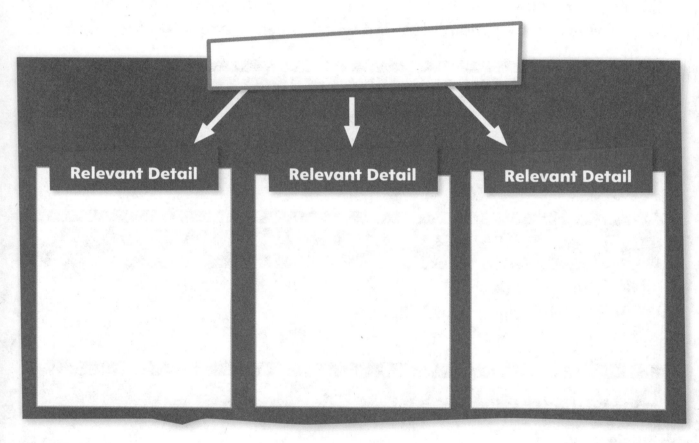

Relevant Detail

Relevant Detail

Relevant Detail

My TURN In your writing notebook, add relevant details to focus and structure your draft of a how-to article.

Ask yourself: Do I really need this detail?

Add Facts and Definitions

In a how-to article, facts and definitions develop the main idea. A fact can be proved. A definition gives the meaning of a word.

In the following paragraph, facts are underlined and words with definitions are highlighted.

Yellowstone National Park is the habitat, or natural home, for many plants and animals. Yellowstone is home to 67 kinds of mammals, including bears and moose. In addition, songbirds and bald eagles live there. A visitor might talk to a ranger, or park caretaker, to learn more about this park's habitat.

My TURN Complete the chart by listing facts and definitions you might include in your article. Place checkmarks next to sources you used.

Facts	Definitions
1. _____ _____	1. _____ _____
2. _____ _____	2. _____ _____
☐ Encyclopedia	☐ Dictionary
☐ Internet	☐ Internet
☐ Other _____	☐ Other _____

My TURN On your own draft, add facts and definitions that support a clear main idea.

Write a Command

How-to articles explain how to do something, so they often contain command sentences. A command sentence tells someone to do something. The subject of a command is "you," but the word *you* is not always written. A command sentence usually ends with a period.

My TURN Change each step of a how-to article in the chart into a command. The first one has been done for you.

How to Grow Plants for Food	
1. Gardeners choose seeds for the vegetables they like to eat.	**1.** Choose seeds for the vegetables you like to eat.
2. Gardeners plant the seeds in soil.	**2.**
3. Gardeners take care of the plants as they grow.	**3.**
4. Gardeners pick vegetables when they are ripe.	**4.**
5. The vegetables should be washed and cooked.	**5.**

My TURN On a draft of your how-to article, write the steps as commands.

Write brief and clear command sentences in a how-to article.

Clarify Steps Using Strong Verbs

When writers clarify how to do something, they provide clear, specific words or additional information to make the steps easier to understand. In a how-to article, strong verbs are clarifying because they tell readers exactly what to do. Strong verbs convey ideas, directions, and information clearly.

My TURN Choose a strong verb from the box to complete each step.

purchase	select	water	research	feed

How to Set Up a Butterfly Garden	
Step 1	_____ which plants butterflies like the most.
Step 2	_____ a location for your garden that has both sunny and shady spots.
Step 3	_____ different kinds of plants and place them in your garden.
Step 4	_____ and _____ your plants to keep them and the butterflies happy!

Discuss with your Writing Club other strong verbs that could be used in the steps. Listen to others' ideas. Ask questions to clarify information.

My TURN On a draft of your how-to article in your writing notebook, use strong verbs to clarify each step.

 INTERACTIVITY

THE FOOD CHAIN

A food chain shows how animals and plants are connected according to the food they eat and the energy they use. Food chains demonstrate how energy moves from the sun to plants to animals. Notice in the diagram how energy from the sun works through the chain to keep the mountain lion alive.

1. SUN The sun is the first link in this food chain. Our sun produces heat, light, and, most important, energy for living things.

2. WILDFLOWERS Plants use the sun's energy to grow. They are called **producers**. They produce, or make, their own food.

Weekly Question

How can a chain of events affect plants and animals?

Quick Write What might happen if the deer or the wildflowers in this food chain disappeared?

4. MOUNTAIN LION Mountain lions are consumers that eat other animals, such as deer.

3. DEER Animals such as deer are **consumers** that consume, or eat, plants. Animals cannot make their own food.

Realistic Fiction

Realistic fiction is a made-up story that is written to engage readers. It includes

- Believable **characters** that can be people or animals
- A **plot** or problem with rising tension or excitement
- A **setting** that could be in real life

TURN and TALK With a partner, describe how realistic fiction is similar to and different from informational text. Use the Realistic Fiction Anchor Chart to help you.

Be a Fluent Reader Fluency includes reading with expression and accuracy. Realistic fiction often contains dialogue between characters, which is good for practicing both expression and accuracy.

When you read dialogue aloud,

○ Raise or lower the pitch of your voice to express the emotion of the character.

○ Read carefully to avoid making mistakes. Use quotation marks to help you group words. Pause when you see a comma or period.

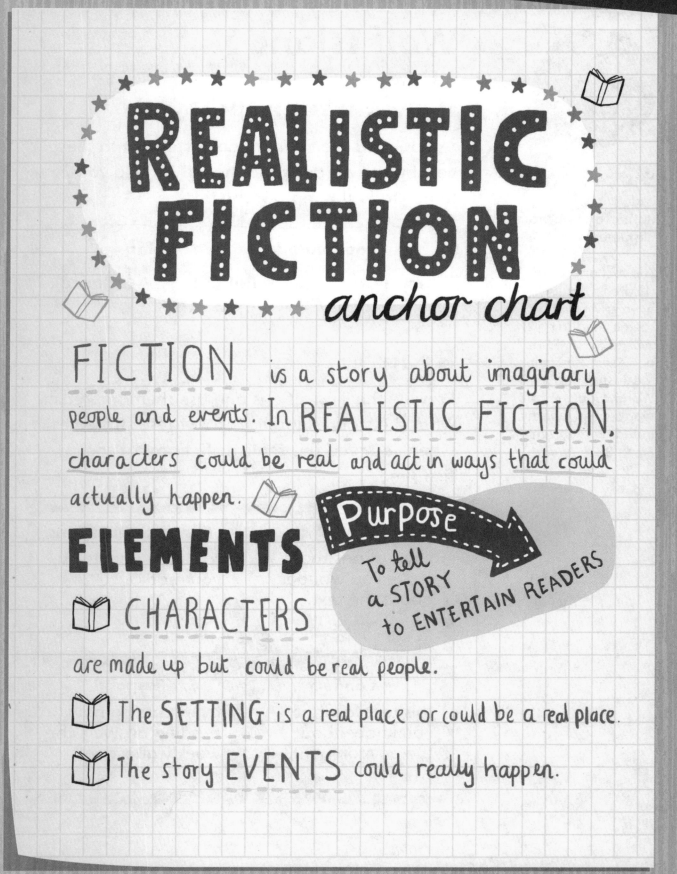

REALISTIC FICTION
anchor chart

FICTION is a story about imaginary people and events. In REALISTIC FICTION, characters could be real and act in ways that could actually happen.

ELEMENTS

Purpose

To tell a STORY to ENTERTAIN READERS

📖 CHARACTERS are made up but could be real people.

📖 The SETTING is a real place or could be a real place.

📖 The story EVENTS could really happen.

Celia Godkin is a biologist, teacher, author, and illustrator best known for her book *Wolf Island*. Some of her children's books have environmental themes, including *The Wolves Return*, *Fire!*, and *Skydiver: Saving the Fastest Bird in the World*. Godkin has won several awards, including the Green Earth Book Award.

Wolf Island

Preview Vocabulary

As you read *Wolf Island*, pay attention to these vocabulary words. Notice how they help you understand the topic of the text.

depended	**well-being**
population	**available**	**balance**

Read

Preview the illustrations and use them to predict what the story is about. Follow these strategies when you read this **realistic fiction** text the first time.

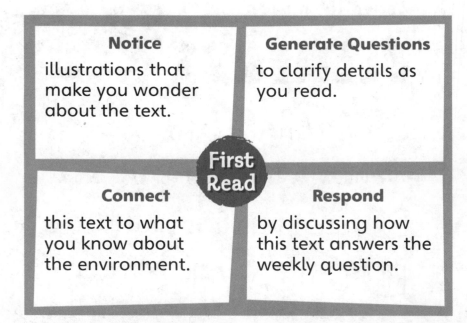

Notice illustrations that make you wonder about the text.

Generate Questions to clarify details as you read.

First Read

Connect this text to what you know about the environment.

Respond by discussing how this text answers the weekly question.

Wolf Island

by Celia Godkin

AUDIO

ANNOTATE

Synthesize Information

Highlight evidence in the text that supports the idea that living things were able to meet their needs on the island.

depended counted or relied on

well-being health and comfort

1   Once there was an island. It was an island with trees and meadows, and many kinds of animals. There were mice, rabbits and deer, squirrels, foxes, and several kinds of birds.

2   All the animals on the island depended on the plants and the other animals for their food and well-being. Some animals ate grass and other plants; some ate insects; some ate other animals. The island animals were healthy. There was plenty of food for all.

3   A family of wolves lived on the island, too—a male wolf, a female, and their five pups.

4   One day, the wolf pups were playing on the beach while their mother and father slept. The pups found a strange object at the edge of the water.

5   It was a log raft, nailed together with boards. The pups had never seen anything like this before. They were very curious.

CLOSE READ

Analyze Illustrations

Look at the illustration on this page. Underline details in the text that this illustration helps you understand.

Analyze Illustrations

Underline important events in the story that are pictured in the illustration.

6   The wolf pups climbed onto the raft and sniffed about. Everything smelled different.

7   While the pups were poking around, the raft began to drift slowly out into the lake. At first the pups didn't notice anything wrong. Then, suddenly, there was nothing but water all around the raft.

8   The pups were scared. They howled. The mother and father wolf heard the howling and came running down to the water's edge.

9   The pups couldn't turn the raft back, and the pups were too scared to swim, so the adult wolves swam out to the raft and climbed aboard. The raft drifted slowly and steadily over to the mainland. Finally, it came to rest on the shore, and the wolf family scrambled onto dry land.

10   There were no longer any wolves on the island.

CLOSE READ

Synthesize Information

Highlight text evidence that you can synthesize with the illustration to help you understand that the island was far from the mainland.

Analyze Illustrations

Underline text details about the animals' winter activities that help you support an appropriate response to this question: What does the illustration help you understand?

11   Time passed. Spring grew into summer on the island, and summer into fall. The leaves turned red. Geese flew south, and squirrels stored up nuts for the winter.

12   Winter was mild that year, with little snow. The green plants were buried under a thin white layer. Deer dug through the snow to find food. They had enough to eat.

13   The next spring, many fawns were born.

14   There were now many deer on the island. They were eating large amounts of grass and leaves. The wolf family had kept the deer population down, because wolves eat deer for food.

15   Without wolves to hunt the deer, there were now too many deer on the island for the amount of food available.

CLOSE READ

Synthesize Information

Highlight text evidence that supports the idea that the island changed because the wolves were gone.

population the number of animals or people living in a place

available ready to use

Synthesize Information

Highlight text evidence that shows that having more deer on the island affects the populations of other animals.

16 Spring grew into summer and summer into fall. More and more deer ate more and more grass and more and more leaves.

17 Rabbits had less to eat, because the deer were eating their food. There were not many baby bunnies born that year.

18 Foxes had less to eat, because there were fewer rabbits for them to hunt.

19 Mice had less to eat, because the deer had eaten the grass and grass seed. There were not many baby mice born that year.

20 Owls had less to eat, because there were fewer mice for them to hunt. Many animals on the island were hungry.

21   The first snow fell. Squirrels curled up in their holes, wrapped their tails around themselves for warmth, and went to sleep. The squirrels were lucky. They had collected a store of nuts for the winter.

22   Other animals did not have winter stores. They had to find food in the snow. Winter is a hard time for animals, but this winter was harder than most. The snow was deep and the weather cold.

23   Most of the plants had already been eaten during the summer and fall. Those few that remained were hard to find, buried deep under the snow.

CLOSE READ

Vocabulary in Context

To determine the meaning of multiple-meaning words, readers use context, or words within the sentence and in nearby sentences, to help them.

The word *store* can mean "a building where goods are sold" or "a supply."

Use context clues within and beyond the sentence to determine the meaning of the word *store* in paragraph 21.

Underline the context clues that support your definition.

Synthesize Information

Highlight text evidence that shows the animals competed for food.

24   Rabbits were hungry. Foxes were hungry. Mice were hungry. Owls were hungry. Even the deer were hungry. The whole island was hungry.

25   The owls flew over to the mainland, looking for mice. They flew over the wolf family walking along the mainland shore.

26   The wolves were thin and hungry, too. They had not found a home, because there were other wolf families on the mainland. The other wolves did not want to share with them.

27 Snow fell for many weeks. The drifts became deeper and deeper. It was harder and harder for animals to find food. Animals grew weaker, and some began to die.

28 The deer were so hungry they gnawed bark from the trees. Trees began to die.

29 Snow covered the island. The weather grew colder and colder. Ice began to form in the water around the island and along the mainland coast. It grew thicker and thicker, spreading farther and farther out into the open water.

Analyze Illustrations

<u>Underline</u> the detail about the deer that the illustration helps you understand.

Analyze Illustrations

Underline a detail in the text that the illustration helps you understand about the wolves' return.

30 One day, the ice reached all the way from the mainland to the island.

31 The wolf family crossed the ice and returned to their old home.

32 The wolves were hungry when they reached the island. There were many weak and sick deer for them to eat. The wolves left the healthy deer alone.

33 Finally, spring came. The snow melted, and grass and leaves began to grow. The wolves remained in their island home, hunting deer. No longer would there be too many deer on the island. Grass and trees would grow again. Rabbits would find enough food. The mice would find enough food. There would be food for the foxes and owls. And there would be food for the deer. The island would have food enough for all.

34 Life on the island was back in balance.

CLOSE READ

Synthesize Information

Highlight a text detail that works with the illustration to help you understand one way the island would recover after the wolves' return.

Fluency Practice reading with accuracy by reading paragraphs 30–34 aloud with a partner. When you come to an unfamiliar word, slow down and try to sound out the word.

balance enough different plants and animals to keep a habitat healthy

Develop Vocabulary

In realistic fiction and other forms of fiction, authors choose words that tie ideas together. The author of *Wolf Island* chose words that describe the connections between the animals and plants that live there.

My TURN With a partner, take turns discussing the meanings of the selection vocabulary words. Listen carefully. Then complete each sentence with the word from the word bank that best fits the meaning and connects the ideas in each box.

Word Bank

available   **balance**   **depended**   **population**   **well-being**

A habitat that is in _____ does not have too many of one kind of animal.

Wolves on the island _____ on deer for food in order to survive.

When the wolves were gone, the _____, or number, of deer became too large for the amount of food _____ on the island.

The _____, or health and comfort, of all animals improved when the wolves came back to Wolf Island.

Check for Understanding

My TURN Look back at the text to answer the questions.

1. How do you know that the story is realistic fiction?

2. How does the description of life on Wolf Island after the wolf family leaves reveal the author's voice?

3. What might have happened to plant and animal life if the wolves had not returned to the island?

4. How could you prove with text evidence that a balance of life on the island is good for all animals and plants on the island?

Analyze Illustrations

Authors use graphic features, such as illustrations, to achieve a specific purpose. **Illustrations** add information and details to a story. They often show the setting, characters, and events and emphasize what the text states.

1. **My TURN** Go to the Close Read notes in *Wolf Island* and underline the parts that help you analyze illustrations.

2. **Text Evidence** Use some of the parts you underlined in the text to complete the chart.

Text Evidence	Illustration Author Uses to Support Text	How Illustration Achieves Author's Purpose
"the raft began to drift slowly out into the lake"	the wolves on the raft, floating away from the island	I understand that the wolf family is floating away from the island.

Synthesize Information

Readers **synthesize,** or combine, the information from both illustrations and words to create new understanding of what they read.

1. **My TURN** Go back to the Close Read notes and highlight evidence that helps you synthesize information.

2. **Text Evidence** Use some of your highlighted text to synthesize information in the story.

Text Evidence	What the Illustration Shows	What I Learned by Synthesizing This Information
"There were now many deer on the island."	deer and fawns	Without wolves to hunt the deer, the number of deer started to grow.

Reflect and Share

Write to Sources Scientists continue to explore relationships among plants and animals. Their work helps us learn more about nature. How do relationships between plants and animals affect the balance of nature? Use evidence from two texts you have read in this unit to write a response to this question.

- -

Interact with Sources Before you start writing, choose a text about balance in nature and another text about how animals survive. Identify passages in the texts that tell you about plant and animal relationships and the balance of nature.

Next, freewrite to identify relevant information in the two texts. To get started, ask yourself questions, such as:

- What do the texts tell me about relationships between plants and animals?
- What details explain how plant and animal relationships affect the balance of nature?

Finally, use your freewriting and details from the texts to write your response on a separate sheet of paper.

- -

Weekly Question

How can a chain of events affect plants and animals?

Academic Vocabulary

Context Clues are words that help you determine the meaning of unfamiliar words. Context clues can be found within and beyond the sentence that contains the unfamiliar word. Once you have used context clues to determine a word's meaning, use a print or digital dictionary or glossary to confirm the meaning.

My TURN For each sentence,

1. **Underline** the academic vocabulary word.

2. **Highlight** the context clue that helps you determine the word's meaning.

3. **Write** a brief definition based on the clues.

The children prefer the south end of the park. They like it better because the playground equipment is the newest and best.

Definition: _____

The city pool has some new features, including a water slide and a diving board.

Definition: _____

Lee must investigate the attic to figure out what the noise is.

Definition: _____

To avoid walking through the mud, they took the long way home.

Definition: _____

Compound Words

Compound Words are two or more words that combine to form a new word. When you read a compound word, read each word within it without a pause between the two words. In the compound word *tugboat*, the two words that are combined are *tug* and *boat*.

My TURN Read each compound word. Then write the two words that are combined to form the compound word.

Compound Word	Two Words	Compound Word	Two Words
everything		anything	
afternoon		campground	
inside		outside	
summertime		doghouse	

High-Frequency Words

High-frequency words are common words that can be difficult to read, and they usually need to be practiced. Read these high-frequency words: *minutes*, *decided*.

Read Like a Writer

Authors write for a purpose: to inform, entertain, or express an opinion. Some authors provide a message in their writing by telling something they think is important.

Model ! Read the sentence from *Wolf Island*.

All the animals on the island depended on the plants and the other animals for their food and well-being.

> important details of the author's message

1. **Identify** Celia Godkin's message talks about how animals depended on the plants.

2. **Question** Why is this detail of the message important?

3. **Conclude** The animals need plants and animals to survive.

Read the passage.

The island would have food enough for all. Life on the island was back in balance.

My TURN Follow the steps to analyze the passage. Identify and explain the author's message.

1. **Identify** Celia Godkin's message is that _____

_____ .

2. **Question** Why is this detail of the message important?

3. **Conclude** This message is important because _____

_____ .

Write for a Reader

Writers have a purpose for writing and often include a message. Many writers feel their message is important to share with others.

Tell why the message is important.

My TURN Think about how Celia Godkin includes details in *Wolf Island* to explain her message about why balance is important. Now write about a message you think is important. Be sure to tell why it is important.

1. Identify a message you think is important.

_____

2. Why do you think this message is important?

_____

_____

3. Write a brief story that tells your message. Be sure to include why the message is important.

_____

_____

_____

_____

_____

_____

Spell Compound Words

Compound Words are two or more words that combine to form a new word. The two words combined in a compound word are spelled the same when they are separate words.

My TURN Read the words. Write the two words that form the compound word. Then spell the compound word.

SPELLING WORDS		
popcorn	airport	outside
football	haircut	playground
moonlight	fireworks	rattlesnake
eyesight		

_____ + _____ = _____   _____ + _____ = _____

_____ + _____ = _____   _____ + _____ = _____

_____ + _____ = _____   _____ + _____ = _____

_____ + _____ = _____   _____ + _____ = _____

_____ + _____ = _____   _____ + _____ = _____

High-Frequency Words

Memorize the spelling of high-frequency words. Write the following high-frequency words on the lines.

minutes _____

decided _____

Singular Possessive Nouns

Recall that a noun names a person, place, or thing. A **singular possessive noun** is a noun that shows that one possesses, or owns, something. To form a singular possessive noun, add an apostrophe and the letter *s* to a singular noun.

Nouns	Singular Possessive Nouns	Examples
doctor	doctor's	the doctor's office
baby	baby's	the baby's toy
dog	dog's	the dog's bone
Ray	Ray's	Ray's computer

My TURN Edit this draft by identifying four nouns that should be singular possessive nouns. Add an apostrophe and the letter *s* to those words.

It was a weird day at practice. Manny ball did not have

enough air in it. So Lamar ran home to borrow his sister

ball. Then Sarah shoe came untied. After that, the coach

whistle broke. Everything seemed to go wrong!

Develop an Introduction

The **introduction** of a how-to article identifies a task or process that will be completed. It gives readers the "big picture" of what the final result will be. An introduction

- Includes an interesting statement that keeps readers wanting to read more
- Tells readers what they will learn
- Gives readers an idea of the organization of the article

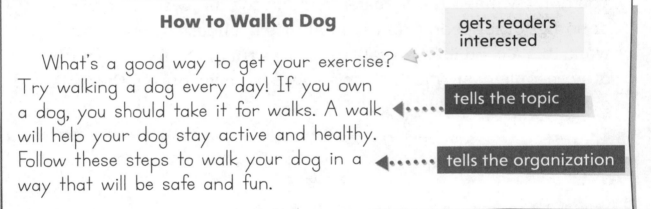

How to Walk a Dog

What's a good way to get your exercise? Try walking a dog every day! If you own a dog, you should take it for walks. A walk will help your dog stay active and healthy. Follow these steps to walk your dog in a way that will be safe and fun.

gets readers interested

tells the topic

tells the organization

My TURN Compose an introduction for your own how-to article. Use the bulleted list above to make sure your introduction contains the right information.

Organize Ideas into Steps

When you think about a task, imagine how to complete it. Organize your ideas into steps. Each step gives one direction to complete a larger task or process. Steps are given in order to provide a structure for readers to follow.

My TURN Write steps from the ideas in this paragraph.

> Dogs like to go for walks. First, decide how far your dog needs to walk. How long does it usually like to be active outside? Then put a leash and a collar on the dog. This will keep the dog safe. You don't want your dog to get lost, run too far away from you, or bother other people and animals. Next, choose a safe place to walk. It is a good idea to walk in an area that is well lit and with other people nearby. If your dog is well behaved during the walk, give it a treat!

1. _____

2. _____

3. _____

4. _____

My TURN On a separate sheet of paper, write ideas for how to finish the task in your how-to article. Then use these ideas to write steps. Compose the middle of your article using these steps.

Organize Steps into Sequence

Steps in a how-to article should be in sequence. Steps should follow one another in a way that makes sense. Group related information into one step. When all steps are in the correct order, the task can be accomplished.

ORGANIZING STEPS

☐ Steps are clear and in the correct order.

☐ Each step contains enough information.

☐ No steps are left out.

My TURN Work with a partner to put the steps in order. Write the number of the step before each sentence. Then compose a final step in the last box.

HOW TO BE A BIRDWATCHER

___ Use your binoculars to watch birds.	___ Go to a park that has a lot of birds.
___ Gather your guidebook and binoculars.	___ **What will you do next?**

My TURN Continue composing your how-to article by grouping related information together and organizing steps into sequence. Use the Organizing Steps checklist to help you.

Add Illustrations

Illustrations, or pictures, can help readers understand your how-to article. Sometimes, only difficult or important steps have illustrations. Other times, every step has one.

My TURN Draw an illustration for the third step in the box. Then compose another step with an illustration.

How to Set Up a Fishbowl

1. Get a bowl.
2. Put rocks on the bottom of the bowl.
3. Fill the bowl with water.

ILLUSTRATIONS

☐ Each illustration has enough detail.

☐ Each illustration supports the text.

My TURN Continue to compose your how-to article by adding illustrations that provide more details.

Add details to illustrations that help readers understand the steps.

Compose a Conclusion

Informative writing ends with a conclusion. A strong conclusion leaves readers feeling positive about what they have learned. It might congratulate readers on finishing all the steps, restate the task that was completed, or tell readers what to do next on their own. As you read this how-to article, notice the focus of the conclusion.

Planting a garden is easy. Plant vegetables you like so you can eat them!

First, clear space in a raised bed or large pot. Then place soil about 3–5 inches high. Next, plant seeds or vegetable plants several inches apart. Water the plants regularly. Finally, harvest your crops when they are ready.

Now you know how to plant a garden! Watch your plants grow, and enjoy the results! You can follow similar steps for planting flowers.

My TURN Compose a conclusion for your how-to article.

My TURN Identify a topic, purpose, and audience. Then select any genre, and plan a draft by freewriting your ideas.

BRINGING ANIMALS Back

An animal may disappear from a particular place due to human activity. Later on, people may help that animal return to its natural habitat.

CALIFORNIA CONDORS

The California condor is the biggest bird in North America. In the 1980s, there were only about 20 left in the world—all living in zoos. In 1992, a few were released back into the wild. Today, more than 400 live in California and nearby areas.

DESERT PUPFISH

The desert pupfish lives in harsh places where other animals cannot easily live. It disappeared from more liveable places when other animals moved in and took over. Today, work is under way to bring the pupfish back.

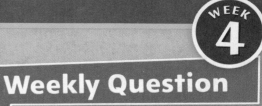

Weekly Question

How does reintroduction of a species affect plants and animals in a habitat?

BIGHORN SHEEP Bighorns are wild sheep that live in the American West. By the 1940s, they had died out in Oregon due to hunting and disease. Scientists brought many back from Canada and other places. Today, there are about 3,500 in Oregon.

Annotate Underline details in the infographic that you think most clearly answer the Weekly Question. Share your work with a partner and explain. Take notes on your discussion.

ARABIAN ORYX An oryx is an antelope that was hunted until only six remained in the wild in 1972. Several countries have worked with zoos to bring the oryx back to Arabia. Today, over 1,000 live in the wild.

Learning Goal

I can learn more about themes concerning *interactions* by analyzing the text structure of persuasive texts.

Persuasive Text

A **persuasive text,** or argumentative text, gives an opinion and develops an argument to support that opinion. Writers of persuasive texts

- Identify the **audience,** or readers they want to convince
- Make a **claim,** or statement of opinion
- Provide **reasons** to support the claim
- Use evidence, examples, and **facts,** not opinions or personal beliefs, to support the reasons
- Use specific words to **appeal to readers' emotions**

What can you say to make me change my opinion?

TURN and TALK   Discuss with a partner how persuasive text is similar to or different from informational text. Use the Persuasive Text Anchor Chart to help you understand persuasive text. Take notes on your discussion.

My **NOTES** _____

_____

_____

_____

_____

PERSUASIVE TEXT
ANCHOR CHART

Types of Persuasive Text

ADVERTISEMENTS promote a product

LETTERS TO THE EDITOR state an opinion or point of view

OPINION ESSAYS argue for or against a topic

Elements of a Strong Argument

- well-organized structure
- a clearly stated claim in the introduction
- reasons that support the claim
- evidence based on research or expert opinion
- a conclusion to sum up the argument

Pooja Makhijani is a writer, editor, and teacher. She lives with her family and many, many books in New Jersey. She formerly lived in Singapore, a city-state in Asia. In her free time, Pooja Makhijani loves to dance, listen to music, and take photos.

Welcome Back, Wolves!

Preview Vocabulary

As you read _Welcome Back, Wolves!_ notice how these vocabulary words relate to the author's argument.

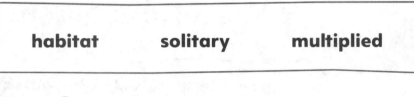

habitat	solitary	multiplied

Read

Establish a purpose for reading persuasive text. Follow these strategies when you read this **persuasive text** the first time.

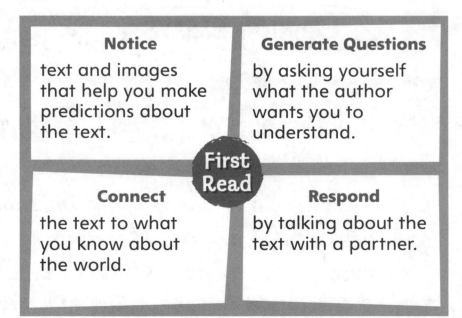

Notice text and images that help you make predictions about the text.

Generate Questions by asking yourself what the author wants you to understand.

First Read

Connect the text to what you know about the world.

Respond by talking about the text with a partner.

Welcome Back, WOLVES !

by Pooja Makhijani

🔊 AUDIO

✏ ANNOTATE

Analyze Text Structure

Underline the sentence that helps you identify the author's claim about wolves in Yellowstone.

habitat the natural home of a plant or animal

1   Yellowstone National Park, with its plentiful food and wide-open spaces, is an ideal habitat for wolves. For many years, though, wolves were banned from the park. The U.S. government thought wolves did more harm than good. Fortunately, the government rethought its decision, and the ban was lifted. Returning wolves to Yellowstone was the right decision for several reasons.

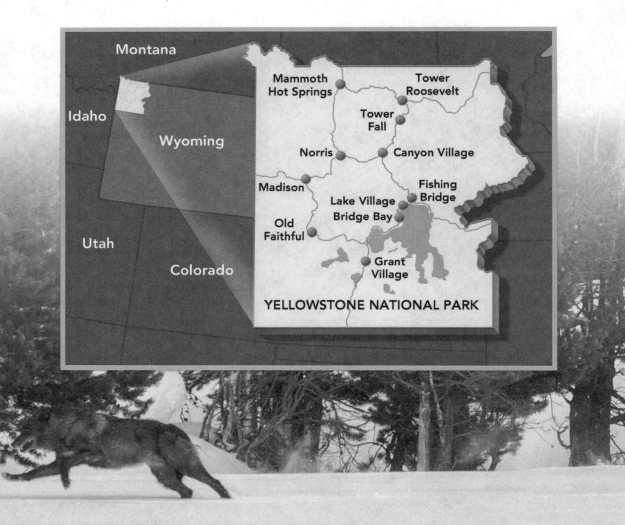

2   In the early 1900s, the U.S. government started a program to control predators in Yellowstone National Park. The government believed wolves and other predators destroyed other park wildlife. Farmers and ranchers supported the program. They said wolves threatened their livestock.

3   To control predators, hunters killed them. By 1926, the last Yellowstone wolf pack had been killed. For decades after that, only a few solitary wolves were sighted.

CLOSE READ

Compare and Contrast Texts

Highlight a key idea about the value of wolves in Yellowstone that contrasts with the information in *Wolves Don't Belong in Yellowstone*.

4   In the 1960s, scientists began to focus on protecting nature rather than controlling it. They wanted to bring wolves back to Yellowstone. Many years later, it happened. By late 2014, there were 104 wolves at the park.

5   As scientists have long realized, wolves improve biodiversity. Biodiversity is the number of species in an ecosystem, or environment. A healthy ecosystem has many different species.

6 When wolves disappeared from Yellowstone, other animals were affected. Elk, wolves' favorite food, multiplied. Elk eat willow trees. Soon, the elk were eating more and more trees. Beavers use willows to make their homes, called dams. Because the elk ate so many trees, beavers didn't have enough wood to build dams. Beavers began to disappear from the park.

7 Then the wolves returned. They began to eat elk. Willows grew back. Beavers returned to the park. As a result, biodiversity improved.

CLOSE READ

Analyze Text Structure

Underline a detail that supports the author's claim that wolves improve biodiversity.

multiplied increased greatly in number

Analyze Text Structure

<u>Underline</u> the author's opinion about the effect of ecotourists who visit Yellowstone.

8   Daniel Licht is one of many scientists who believe wolves help Yellowstone. "We have these ecosystems that are in dire need of wolves," said Licht. He thinks wolves should be returned to other habitats, too. "The pros, the benefits, would far outweigh the negatives," he said.

9   Bringing wolves back to Yellowstone has helped in another way. Wolves bring ecotourists to the park. Ecotourists are people who travel to see nature.

10   Ecotourists come from around the world to see Yellowstone's wolves. A 2006 study found that ecotourists spend millions of dollars in and around the park area each year. Some of that money goes to restaurants and hotels. In other words, wolves help people pay their bills. That's a *good* thing!

11 The return of wolves has been important for a third reason. It has helped prove that wolves and people can live together in peace.

12 No wolf has attacked a human at Yellowstone. And studies show that only a tiny percent of livestock die from wolf attacks. The "big, bad wolf" is a myth.

13 Wolves belong at Yellowstone. Now that they're back, nature is in balance. Tourism is up, too. Predators such as wolves always bring some dangers. However, the good they do far outweighs the risks. Welcome back, wolves!

CLOSE READ

Compare and Contrast Texts

Highlight details that suggest that the author's purpose for writing this text is different from the author's purpose for writing *Wolves Don't Belong in Yellowstone.*

Frances Ruffin has written more than 40 books for children. She says, "I cannot remember a time when I did not read. I love reading, researching, and writing something new. My favorite quotation comes from children's book author Walter Dean Meyers: 'Once I began to read, I began to exist.'"

Wolves Don't Belong in Yellowstone

Preview Vocabulary

As you read *Wolves Don't Belong in Yellowstone*, pay attention to how the author uses these vocabulary words in her argument.

> **eliminated**   **reintroduced**

Read and Compare

Before you begin, ask yourself, "How does the argument in this text compare to that in the previous text?" Readers of **persuasive texts** follow these strategies when they first read a text.

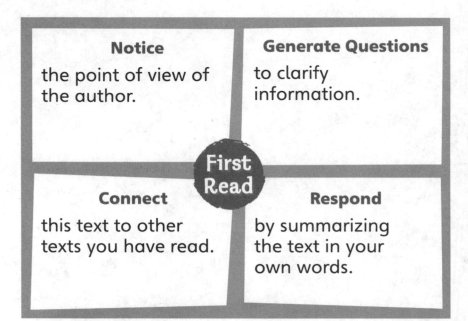

Notice the point of view of the author.

Generate Questions to clarify information.

First Read

Connect this text to other texts you have read.

Respond by summarizing the text in your own words.

WOLVES
DON'T BELONG
in Yellowstone

by Frances Ruffin

AUDIO

ANNOTATE

Analyze Text Structure

<u>Underline</u> the sentence that helps you identify the author's claim about wolves in Yellowstone.

eliminated removed

1   Gray wolves are too dangerous to roam in Yellowstone National Park. That's why the government eliminated most wolves from the park in the early 1900s. Removing the wolves was the right decision.

2   However, in the 1960s, scientists began arguing for the wolves' return. Wolves would bring more biodiversity to Yellowstone, they said.

3   Many people loved the idea of having wolves in the park again. To them, wolves are predators to admire. They're powerful, intelligent animals.

4   The pro-wolf side won. Today, wolves are back in Yellowstone. And they're as dangerous as they ever were.

5   Farmers and ranchers speak most loudly against wolves in Yellowstone. To them, wolves are bad news.

6   Wolves often wander outside their Yellowstone habitat. They end up on nearby lands. Those lands include many farms and ranches. Most farms and ranches have cattle and other livestock.

CLOSE READ

Compare and Contrast Texts

Highlight a key detail about farmers and ranchers that is the same in both texts.

355

Vocabulary in Context

Use a context clue beyond the sentence to determine the meaning of *alert*.

Underline the context clue that supports your definition.

7   According to many ranchers, wolves create a "landscape of fear." Cattle stay on the alert while grazing. They spend less time eating and more time looking around for danger. As a result, they eat less. They fail to gain weight.

8   When ranchers sell their cattle, they get a higher price for fatter cattle. If cattle fail to gain weight, ranchers make less money.

9 Doug Smith is Wolf Project Leader at Yellowstone. He wanted wolves back at Yellowstone. But even he says, "Life is simpler without wolves. I admit that if you are a rancher, having wolves around is worrisome. I understand that it's not just the cows they kill; it's the sleepless nights. I think that's the best argument to not have them."

CLOSE READ

Analyze Text Structure

<u>Underline</u> the statements in the quote by Doug Smith that are opinions, not facts.

Analyze Text Structure

Underline claims you identify that are meant to persuade readers that wolves in Yellowstone cause problems.

10   There's another problem too. Wolves increase Yellowstone's grizzly bear population. Grizzlies are scavengers. They eat the prey wolves leave behind. When there are more wolves, grizzlies have more prey to scavenge.

11   Hungry grizzlies often eat from garbage dumps and campsites. This increases the chance they'll come face to face with people. Grizzlies are far more likely to attack people than wolves are.

12   Finally, in spite of all the debate, wolves may not improve Yellowstone's ecosystem. Scientists have said that wolves were needed to reduce the elk herd. When there were no wolves, the elk herd grew. Elk eat tree leaves. Some trees suffered when the elk herd grew. After wolves were reintroduced, the elk herd decreased. The trees started to recover. Some scientists, however, say that the trees were simply suffering from drought. Maybe the wolves didn't help them after all.

13   Wolves are not the answer to Yellowstone's problems. Instead, they bring new problems. Yellowstone National Park would be better off without them.

CLOSE READ

Compare and Contrast Texts

Highlight key details of the author's message that contrast with the author's message in *Welcome Back, Wolves!*

reintroduced brought an animal or plant back into an area

Develop Vocabulary

Authors often use synonyms to provide variety in their writing. They also use antonyms to show the opposite of an idea.

My TURN Review each vocabulary word in the texts. Identify a synonym and antonym for each word and explain its meaning by writing its definition. Then, work with a partner to use each synonym and antonym in a sentence of your own.

Synonym	Vocabulary Word	Antonym
	solitary	
	multiplied	
	eliminated	
	reintroduced	

Check for Understanding

My TURN Look back at the text to answer the questions.

1. How can the reader identify both texts as persuasive texts?

2. How does each author use photographs to support the argument for or against wolves in Yellowstone Park?

3. What conclusion can you draw about each author's attitude toward wolves in Yellowstone Park?

4. Which author does a better job of persuading readers about her topic? Use evidence from each text to support your opinion.

Analyze Text Structure

Authors of persuasive texts structure their writing in special ways. These authors make a claim, or state an opinion, and support the claim with reasons. Authors must use facts, not opinions or personal beliefs, to support their claims. The goal is to get the audience, or the readers they are trying to convince, to agree with their side of the argument.

1. **My TURN** Go to the Close Read notes and underline parts that relate to text structure.

2. **Text Evidence** Use some of the parts you underlined to complete the graphic organizer.

Welcome Back, Wolves!

Claim: "Returning wolves to Yellowstone was the right decision"

Audience: readers who do not want wolves in the park or who are undecided

Wolves Don't Belong in Yellowstone

Claim:

Audience:

Facts and Opinions That Support Makhijani's Claim

Fact: "the wolves returned. They began to eat elk. Willows grew back. Beavers returned"

Opinion: "That's a *good* thing!"

Facts and Opinions That Support Ruffin's Claim

Fact:

Opinion:

Compare and Contrast Texts

Authors use persuasive words to convince readers to agree with their point of view. You can compare and contrast the important points and key details that authors use to support their opinions.

1. 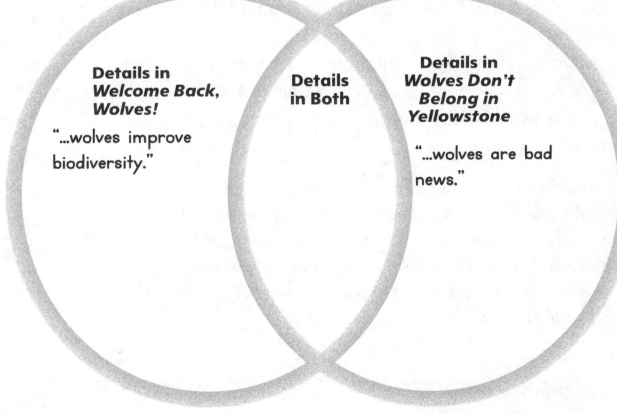 **My TURN** Go back to the Close Read notes in the two persuasive texts. Highlight details that help you compare and contrast the texts.

2. **Text Evidence** Use some of the highlighted text to compare and contrast the two texts. Then evaluate the details you chose to determine the main idea of each text.

Details in Welcome Back, Wolves!

"...wolves improve biodiversity."

Details in Both

Details in Wolves Don't Belong in Yellowstone

"...wolves are bad news."

Main Idea of Welcome Back, Wolves!:

_____

Main Idea of Wolves Don't Belong in Yellowstone:

_____

Reflect and Share

Write to Sources In this unit, you have read about different habitats and their effects on animals and plants. Think about what makes a habitat healthy for living things. Then write an opinion about what makes a healthy habitat. Include evidence from the texts to support your opinion.

Use Text Evidence Support your opinion with text evidence. Evidence might be facts, reasons, or examples. Ask yourself these questions to help you find the best supporting evidence.

- Does this evidence contain facts, reasons, or examples?
- Does this evidence support my opinion?
- Will this evidence help convince others to agree with my opinion?

Write a sentence that states your opinion about what a healthy habitat is like. Then choose two texts you have read in this unit. Find supporting evidence from each text. Use the questions to decide whether or not to include the evidence to support your opinion. On a separate sheet of paper, write a paragraph that supports your opinion.

Weekly Question

How does reintroduction of a species affect plants and animals in a habitat?

Academic Vocabulary

Figurative language gives words a meaning beyond their usual, everyday definitions. One type of figurative language is a simile, which compares two things using the word *like* or *as*.

 For each sentence below,

1. Read each underlined simile.

2. Match the word in the word bank with the simile that best relates to the word's definition.

3. Choose two of the similes. Then write two sentences that each include a simile and its related academic vocabulary word.

Word Bank

prefer	features	investigate	associate

The cheering <u>sounds</u>, <u>like music to my ears</u>, reminded me of scoring the big goal. _____

They <u>look</u> for evidence <u>as thoroughly as a detective</u> in order to solve the mystery. _____

The <u>petals, stems, and leaves</u> of the flowers are <u>as pretty as a rainbow</u>.

_____

They <u>would rather run like the wind</u> than walk. _____

_____

_____

_____

Syllable Patterns

Syllable Pattern VC*e*, or *vowel-consonant-e*, is a syllable with a long vowel sound. The silent *e* at the end signals that the first vowel in the syllable is long. For example, the word *Yellowstone* in paragraph 1 of *Welcome Back, Wolves!* has the VCe syllable pattern. The silent *e* at the end of the word signals that the *o* in the last syllable is long.

My TURN Read each word with syllable pattern VCe in the box. Write the words in the correct column based on the VCe syllable pattern.

ignite	trombone	excite	attitude	relate
locate	excuse	complete	explode	concrete

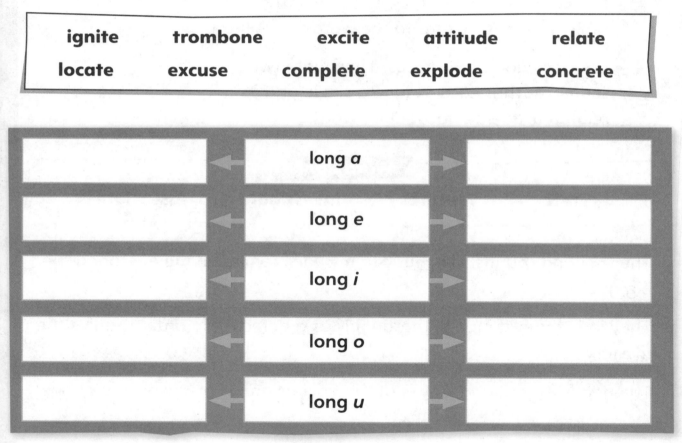

long *a*

long *e*

long *i*

long *o*

long *u*

High-Frequency Words

High-frequency words appear often in text but may not follow regular sound-spelling patterns. Read these high-frequency words: *fact, course*.

Read Like a Writer

Authors use words in a specific way to reveal their voice, or personality. **Tone** is the author's attitude toward the subject. For example, an author may use words in a particular way to create a serious or funny tone.

Model ! Read the sentence from *Welcome Back, Wolves!*

"We have these ecosystems that are in dire need of wolves," said Licht.

word choice

1. **Identify** The words *dire need* create a serious tone.

2. **Question** How does this tone contribute to the author's voice?

3. **Conclude** The serious tone lets the reader know that the author believes that wolves are critical to the ecosystem.

Read the passage.

In other words, wolves help people pay their bills. That's a *good* thing!

My TURN Follow the steps to analyze the passage. Describe how tone helps to reveal the author's voice.

1. **Identify** The word _____ in _____ creates a positive tone.

2. **Question** How does this tone contribute to the author's voice?

3. **Conclude** The positive tone lets the reader know that the author believes _____
_____
_____ .

Write for a Reader

Choose words that show how you feel.

Use language that shows your voice, or personality, in a text. One way to help readers identify your voice is to relay your tone, or attitude, toward a topic.

My TURN In *Welcome Back, Wolves!* Pooja Makhijani uses language in a purposeful way to express her strong opinion against banning wolves from the park. Identify how you can choose particular words to create a tone and show your voice.

1. Think of a subject you feel strongly about. Write the subject and tell how you feel about it.

    Subject:

    _____

    My Feelings:

    _____

    _____

2. Write about your subject. Choose words that create a tone and show your voice. Discuss how your use of language contributes to your voice.

    _____

    _____

    _____

    _____

    _____

Spell Words with Syllable Patterns

Words with the Syllable Pattern VCe can be multisyllabic, or more than one syllable. A long vowel sound is spelled with a single vowel, followed by a consonant and the letter e, which does not spell a sound at all.

My TURN Sort each VCe word by its long vowel spelling and sound.

SPELLING WORDS

compete	expose	reptile
despite	include	subscribe
dispute	mistake	translate
explode		

long _a_ ➡	
long _e_ ➡	
long _i_ ➡	
long _o_ ➡	
long _u_ ➡	

High-Frequency Words

Write the following high-frequency words on the lines.

fact _____

course _____

Plural Possessive Nouns

A **plural possessive noun** shows that two or more people share or own something.

- To form the possessive of a plural noun, add an apostrophe to plural nouns that end in *-s*, *-es*, or *-ies*.
- To form possessives of plural nouns that do not end in *-s*, *-es*, or *-ies*, add an apostrophe and an *s*.

Nouns	Plural Possessive Nouns
scientists	the **scientists'** boots
wolves	the **wolves'** den
puppies	the **puppies'** mother
children	the **children's** backpacks

My TURN Edit this draft by adding an apostrophe or an apostrophe and the letter *s* to form plural possessive nouns.

It was a snowy day at Yellowstone. Several bobcats huddled in their den. The bobcats den was covered in three feet of snow. The kittens fur and body heat helped them stay warm. Outside the den, the campers jackets kept them warm as they marched down the trail.

Edit for Prepositions and Prepositional Phrases

A **preposition** shows a relationship, or connection, between a noun or pronoun and other words in a sentence. Some examples follow:

above	across	after	around	at
before	by	for	from	in

A **prepositional phrase** begins with a preposition and ends with a noun or pronoun.

Preposition	Prepositional Phrase	Sentence
around	around the corner	I live **around the corner**.
for	for days	He studied **for days**.
with	with me	Dee walks **with me**.

My TURN Use prepositions to complete the sentences.

1. A small pond is _____ my house.

2. Ducks move _____ the water.

3. Fish swim _____ the water.

4. The habitat is good _____ animals.

My TURN Edit a draft of your how-to article for prepositions.

Revising for Coherence and Clarity

Writers want their writing to be coherent and clear so readers can understand their ideas. Writing has **coherence** when it holds together in an organized way. Writing has **clarity** when it is easy to follow and understand.

Writers revise for coherence and clarity so readers can understand their ideas. Revision may include adding linking words and phrases to guide readers through the text. Some common linking words include *and*, *but*, *more*, *also*, and *another*.

My TURN Revise the draft for coherence and clarity by adding linking words and phrases.

1. Add two linking words from the Word Bank to the paragraph.
2. Add the phrase *these steps* to a sentence.
3. Combine two sentences with the word *and*.

Word Bank

another	also	but	more

How to Welcome a New Dog

When you bring home a new dog, take these steps so it feels welcomed and loved. Give it its own bed. Give it its own food dish. Take it outside regularly. Give it lots of exercise. A good trick is to introduce your new dog to your other pets slowly. Make sure they get along. If you follow, your new dog will feel at home in no time!

My TURN Edit a draft of your how-to article for coherence and clarity by adding linking words and phrases.

Edit for Nouns

A **noun** names a person, place, or thing. A **singular noun** names *one* person, place, or thing. A **plural noun** names *more than one* person, place, or thing.

Singular	Change	Plural
lion	add -*s*	lions
box	add -*es*	boxes
cherry	change *y* to *i*, add -*es*	cherries
person	irregular plural	people

A **common noun** names *any* person, place, or thing: *day, holiday*.
A **proper noun** names a *particular* person, place, or thing and begins with a capital letter: *Monday, Fourth of July*.

My TURN Edit the paragraph to show the correct form of four nouns. Spell each word correctly.

Many peoples think it is important to care for trees. Trees make the Air healthier to breathe. They give protection from sun and rain. Many animals also make home and find food in trees. When people care for trees, they help the entire Planet!

My TURN Edit a draft of your how-to article for singular, plural, common, and proper nouns.

Edit for Adverbs

An **adverb** is a word that modifies a verb and tells *how* or *when*. Writers use adverbs that tell *how* or *when* to describe actions.

Adverbs that tell **how** something happens or happened are called adverbs of manner. These adverbs often end in *-ly*.

Sentence	Adverb	Verb	Meaning
The number of wolves grew **quickly**.	quickly	grew	**How** did the number of wolves grow? Quickly.
Scientists **closely** watch animal behavior.	closely	watch	**How** do scientists watch? Closely.

Adverbs of time tell **when** something will happen or did happen.

Sentence	Adverb	Verb	Meaning
He visited the park **yesterday**.	yesterday	visited	**When** did he visit the park? Yesterday.
Soon, new trees will be planted in the habitat.	soon	will be planted	**When** will new trees be planted? Soon.

My TURN Complete each sentence with an adverb of time or manner.

1. Ted spoke _____ .

2. The audience listened _____ .

3. _____ we will visit.

4. Our vacation _____ arrived.

My TURN Edit a draft of your how-to article for adverbs that convey time and manner.

Edit for Coordinating Conjunctions

A **conjunction** is a word that connects words or groups of words. The **coordinating conjunctions** are *and*, *but*, and *or*.

Original Sentences	Conjunction	Compound Subject (two or more subject parts)
Wolves live in the forest. Deer live in the forest.	**and** (adds more information)	Wolves **and** deer live in the forest.

Original Sentences	Conjunction	Compound Predicate (two or more predicate parts)
These plants help birds. These plants do not attract butterflies.	**but** (shows a difference)	These plants help birds **but** do not attract butterflies.

Original Sentences	Conjunction	Compound Sentence (two or more complete sentences joined by a comma and a coordinating conjunction)
The animals will live peacefully. They will fight for food and territory.	**or** (shows a choice)	The animals will live peacefully, **or** they will fight for food and territory.

My TURN Edit your how-to article for coordinating conjunctions to combine subjects, predicates, or sentences. Then meet with your Writing Club to share and discuss your changes. Read your article aloud to the Writing Club, and discuss why you chose the coordinating conjunctions you used.

 INTERACTIVITY

PLANTS and ANIMALS
Need Each Other

A food chain shows how each living thing gets food and how energy is passed from one animal to another. A food web is a number of connected food chains.

This marine food web shows how plants and animals in an Alaskan habitat depend on one another. Every habitat has its own plant and animal web. For instance, in the desert, animals use plants such as the cactus for water and shade. The plants need animals to spread seed and pollen.

Salmon and **sand lance** fish eat zooplankton.

Phytoplankton are microscopic plants in oceans. They are producers because they make their own food.

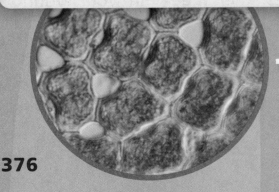

Zooplankton are tiny animals in the ocean that eat phytoplankton.

Weekly Question

Why is it important for plants and animals to depend on each other?

✏️**Illustrate** Look at the marine food web diagram. Review what you have read so far in this unit, and think about how people are part of a food web. Next, draw a different food web that includes you. Show some of the plants and animals you eat. Label your diagram.

The **rat** and **fox**, small land animals, eat the puffin.

A **puffin** is a small seabird that eats the salmon and sand lance.

Learning Goal

I can learn more about informational texts and explain the author's purpose in an informational text.

Spotlight on Genre

Informational Text

Writers of **informational text** include features that help readers understand facts and details.

These features may include

- **Organizational aids**, such as sections, headings, a glossary, or an index
- **Time lines**, **graphs**, or **other features** to help readers visualize information
- **Captions**, **labels**, or **sidebars** to provide additional information
- **Bold** or **italicized words**
- **Numbered** or **bulleted lists** to separate pieces of information

Wow! You can learn a lot of interesting facts by reading informational texts!

TURN and TALK Think about an informational text you have read. With a partner, discuss the author's use of print, graphic, and other characteristic features of informational text. Use the Features of Informational Text Anchor Chart to guide your discussion. Take notes on your discussion.

My NOTES

378

FEATURES OF INFORMATIONAL TEXT ANCHOR CHART

✓ **GRAPHIC AIDS PROVIDE ADDITIONAL DETAILS**

Examples: maps, charts, diagrams, tables, photographs, illustrations, sidebars.

✓ **ORGANIZATIONAL AIDS HELP READERS FIND TOPICS, WORDS, AND DEFINITIONS**

Examples: table of contents, index, glossary.

✓ **STYLE ELEMENTS CALL ATTENTION TO IMPORTANT DETAILS**

Examples: bold print, italic type, headings, labels.

Mary Miché has made several collections of songs for children, including *Nature Nuts*, *Peace It Together*, and *Kid's Stuff*. She is also the author of *Weaving Music into Young Minds*, a textbook for adults on how to teach music to young people.

Nature's Patchwork Quilt

Preview Vocabulary

As you read *Nature's Patchwork Quilt*, pay attention to these vocabulary words. Notice how they clarify information in the text.

interdependence	**food chain**
camouflage **adaptations**	**biodiversity**

Read

Before you begin, preview the illustrations, and think about how they relate to the title of the text. Follow these strategies when you read this **informational text** the first time.

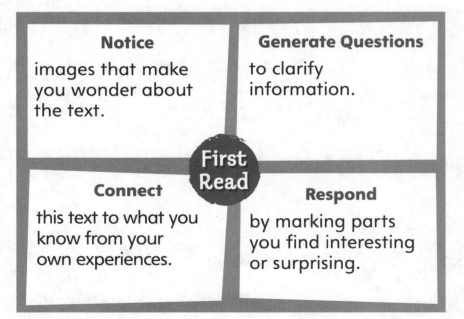

Notice images that make you wonder about the text.

Generate Questions to clarify information.

Connect this text to what you know from your own experiences.

Respond by marking parts you find interesting or surprising.

First Read

Genre **Informational Text**

Nature's Patchwork Quilt

Understanding Habitats

by Mary Miché

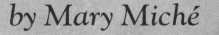

🔊 AUDIO

✐ ANNOTATE

Explain Author's Purpose

Underline a detail the author uses to describe the topic of nature. How do the details help explain the author's purpose and message?

1   Look into nature and you will see a patchwork of beauty and mystery.

2   A patchwork quilt has many pieces that fit together to make a beautiful blanket.

3   Nature is like a patchwork quilt. It has many different habitats all pieced together to create our wonderful planet.

CLOSE READ

Visualize Details

Highlight details that help you create a mental image of how nature is like a patchwork quilt. Describe how this imagery helps the author achieve a specific purpose.

Visualize Details

Highlight a simile. Explain how the simile conveys the author's purpose of helping the reader create a mental image of the interdependence of plants and animals.

interdependence when things depend or rely on one another

4   In a habitat, such as a forest, animals and plants live together. They are food for each other and help the forest grow and develop.

5   Each plant or animal depends on others, like a quilt stitched together. We call this interdependence.

6   A desert is another habitat, with plants and animals that can live in a hot and dry climate.

7   In a quilt, each piece has its own unique place in the design. In a habitat, each animal and plant has a special role, called its niche.

CLOSE READ

Explain Author's Purpose

Underline details that describe the similarity between quilts and habitats. How does this comparison help explain the author's message?

Vocabulary in Context

The word *roots* can mean "plant parts that grow underground" or "digs up."

<u>Underline</u> context clues within the sentence that tell you the meaning of the word *roots* in this text.

food chain a series of living things that depend on each other as food sources

8   A prairie is a grassland habitat. Some prairies have prairie dogs that eat roots and plants. Snakes eat the prairie dogs. Hawks eat the snakes.

9   This is called a food chain. The prairie plants are the first link, prairie dogs are second, snakes are third, and hawks, at the top of the food chain, are the fourth link.

10   The ocean, which has 97% of all the water on Earth, has many different habitats. Ocean water near the surface contains very tiny plants called phytoplankton.

11   Tiny animals called zooplankton eat phytoplankton. Tiny shrimp called krill eat zooplankton. Little fish called sardines eat krill. Salmon eat sardines. Sharks or seals eat salmon. This is one marine food chain.

Explain Author's Purpose

<u>Underline</u> details that help explain and support the author's message that the ocean has unique habitats with food chains.

Visualize Details

Highlight details that help you create a mental image of the adaptations of birds and fish. Explain how these details help deepen your understanding of the text.

camouflage hide or make harder to see in one's natural surroundings

adaptations changes in plants and animals that help them survive

12   The seashore at the edge of the ocean also has many habitats. Different plants and animals live in the shallow water, on the rocks, and in the sand.

13   Over generations, plants and animals often change in ways that help them survive. For instance, the feet of swimming birds changed to have webbing, which help them swim better than their ancestors did. Some fish can change colors to help them hide, or camouflage, themselves. Such changes are called adaptations.

14 Lakes and ponds have many tiny plants and animals living in them. They are very small, but you can see them with a magnifying glass or a special tool called a microscope.

15 These microscopic plants and animals are food for each other. The way that these plants and animals eat and are eaten is so complicated that we call it a food web.

CLOSE READ

Explain Author's Purpose

Underline the author's key ideas about small plants and animals in lakes and ponds. How do these details help explain the author's purpose and message?

CLOSE READ

Vocabulary in Context

The word *burrows* can mean "holes in the ground that animals use for shelter" or "dig a hole to hide in."

<u>Underline</u> context clues within the sentence that tell you the meaning of the word *burrows* in this text.

16 Arctic and high mountain habitats are very cold much of the year. It's a tough place to live. To survive harsh climates, plants either stay alive all winter under snow or make seeds that can survive the cold.

17 Animals store up food to survive in burrows or hibernate in caves. Birds fly to warmer places. Ways of adjusting to the climate are called survival mechanisms.

18   Rainforest habitats are very wet. Cool rainforests are temperate, such as in North America and New Zealand. Hot rainforests are tropical, such as in South America, Africa, and southern Asia.

19   Many rainforest trees are large. Many are cut down. This is called deforestation. Fewer places are left for plants and animals that can only survive in a rainforest.

20   Rainforests have lots and lots and LOTS of different kinds of trees, shrubs, mosses, lichens, fungi, insects, reptiles, amphibians, birds and mammals. Many different species together make up biodiversity.

CLOSE READ

Visualize Details

Highlight text details that help you create a mental image of the different living things found in rainforests. Explain how these mental images deepen your understanding of biodiversity.

biodiversity the existence of many different kinds of plants and animals in an environment

Explain Author's Purpose

Underline details that help the reader understand changes caused by people. Evaluate these details to help you determine the key idea of paragraphs 21 and 22.

21   Houses, towns, and cities are habitats for people. People built them over what once was a prairie, desert, forest, or rainforest. People have changed some plants and animals by working with them over generations.

22   Dogs, cats, and farm animals, as well as many plants that produce food, are very different from their wild ancestors. When plants and animals are changed by people we call it domestication.

23   Ranches and farms are also habitats made by people on what was once prairie, forest, or desert. Often domesticated animals like cows, horses, pigs, and chickens live there. Domesticated plants like tomatoes, corn, and wheat also grow there.

24   More and more natural habitats are being taken over by human habitats. When a natural habitat is gone and plants or animals don't have any place left to live, they die. When the last plant or animal of a species dies, the species is extinct.

Visualize Details

Highlight details that help the reader create mental images of the work environmentalists do. Tell how these mental images deepen your understanding of the importance of preserving habitats.

25   Because plants and animals can't speak for themselves, many environmentalists have worked hard to save them by preserving their habitats.

26   They clean up rivers, plant trees, help animals, study science, paint pictures, sing songs, write books, give speeches, make movies, persuade policy-makers, give money, organize friends, and much more.

27   When you are in nature, look around at its beauty. Consider how all the plants and animals live together in an interdependent web of life.

28   This patchwork quilt of nature covers the whole Earth, your home. It is yours to learn about, to enjoy, to care for, and to love.

Explain Author's Purpose

Underline details that provide clues about how the author wants readers to think and feel about Earth. How do these details contribute to the author's purpose and message within the text?

Develop Vocabulary

In informational text, authors use specific words to explain a topic. When authors write about scientific topics, such as habitats and nature, they may use scientific words to inform readers about the topic.

My TURN Look at the word at the top of each box. In the box, write a sentence to show how that word relates to habitats.

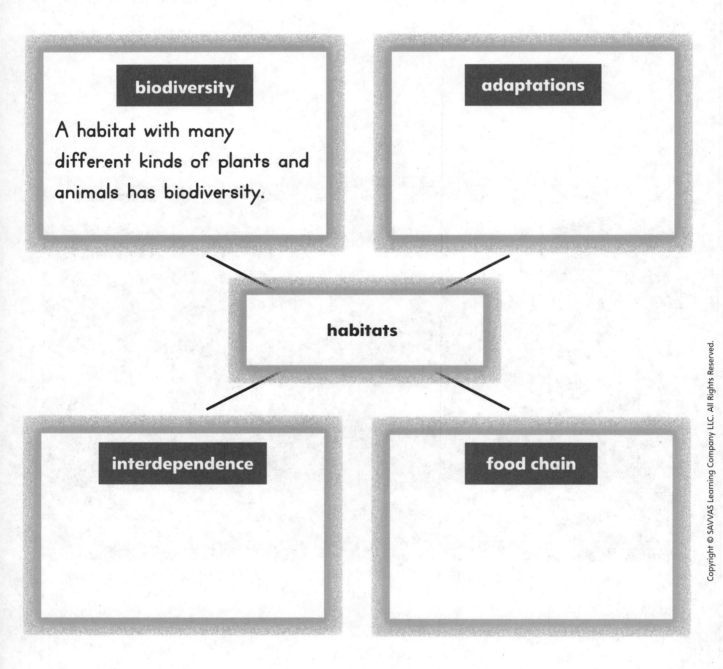

biodiversity

A habitat with many different kinds of plants and animals has biodiversity.

adaptations

habitats

interdependence

food chain

Check for Understanding

My TURN Look back at the text to answer the questions.

1. How can the reader tell that *Nature's Patchwork Quilt* is informational text?

2. Why does the author compare habitats to a patchwork quilt? Use this comparison to explain the author's purpose and message within the text.

3. How do survival mechanisms help animals and plants survive in cold climates? Cite text evidence.

4. When people take over a habitat, how can they affect the animals and plants in that habitat? Use text evidence to support your response.

Explain Author's Purpose

An **author's purpose** is his or her reason for writing. Identifying the author's purpose helps readers understand the message, or meaning, of the text.

1. **My TURN** Go to the Close Read notes in *Nature's Patchwork Quilt*. Underline the parts that relate to the author's purpose.

2. **Text Evidence** Use some of the parts you underlined to complete the chart.

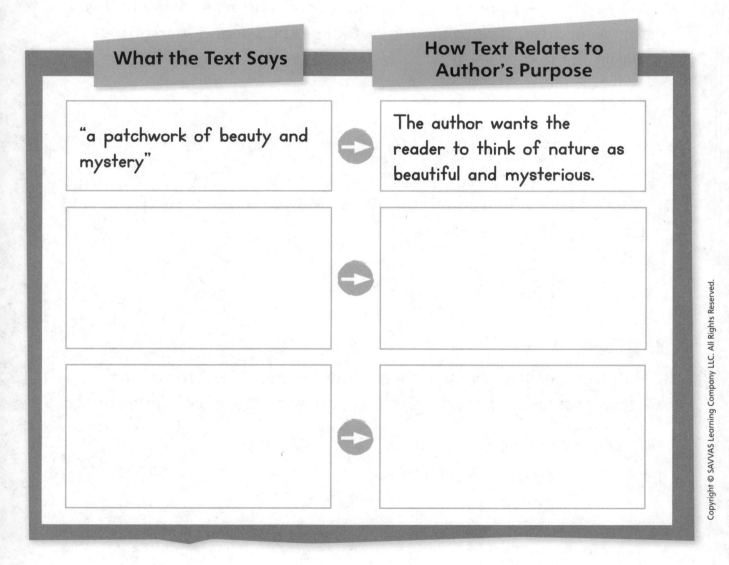

What the Text Says		How Text Relates to Author's Purpose
"a patchwork of beauty and mystery"	→	The author wants the reader to think of nature as beautiful and mysterious.
	→	
	→	

Visualize Details

Authors use descriptive details and imagery to create vivid mental images in readers' minds. These mental pictures deepen readers' understanding of the text and allow them to better understand the author's purpose.

1. **My TURN** Go back to the Close Read notes and highlight evidence related to visualizing details.

2. **Text Evidence** Use some of the highlighted text to complete the chart.

Author's Imagery	What I Picture	How It Achieves Author's Purpose
"many different habitats all pieced together"	I imagine each habitat as a separate patch in a quilt that covers Earth.	The image helps the reader picture habitats on Earth as different but connected.

Reflect and Share

Talk About It In this unit, you read about many different habitats. Animals and plants depend on their habitat to survive. Should people protect natural habitats? Discuss your opinion and support it using details from the texts.

Make Thoughtful Comments Before you comment during a discussion, be sure it is related to the topic. Remember to

- ◎ stay on the topic.
- ◎ build on each other's comments.
- ◎ ask questions about ideas you do not understand.

Use these sentence starters to guide your comments to make sure they are meaningful.

I disagree with you for this reason: . . .

Please explain your comment about . . .

Weekly Question

Why is it important for plants and animals to depend on each other?

Academic Vocabulary

Parts of Speech are categories of words: nouns, verbs, adjectives, adverbs, pronouns, interjections, conjunctions, and prepositions. Some words might be more than one part of speech.

Noun: We will take a spelling *test* on Friday.

Verb: Teachers *test* students to check understanding.

My TURN For each sentence below,

1. **Read** each sentence and underline the academic vocabulary word.

2. **Identify** the word's part of speech.

3. **Write** your own sentence using the word as a different part of speech. You may need to use it as a base word or add to the base word. For example, *avoidance* includes the suffix *-ance*.

Sentence	Part of Speech	My Sentence
The dogs <u>prefer</u> to play in the cooler weather.	verb	His preference is fall over winter. (noun)
I <u>associate</u> that memory with Grandma.		
The <u>features</u> of the statue look so realistic.		
Detectives <u>investigate</u> the scene.		
We <u>avoid</u> taking the long way home.		

Contractions

Contractions are shortened forms of two words. An apostrophe (') shows where letters have been left out. Some contractions can be read using regular spellings, such as the word *it's*. Other contractions need to be practiced so you know how to read them, such as the word *can't*.

My TURN

1. Read these contractions: *I'm*, *I've*, *she's*, *they're*, *we've*.

2. Combine the words in each row and write the contraction.

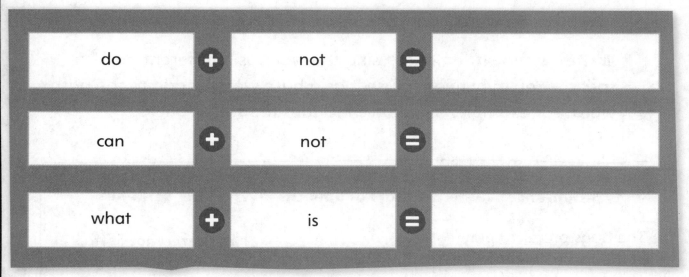

High-Frequency Words

High-frequency words often do not follow regular word study patterns. Read these high-frequency words: *contain*, *front*.

Read Like a Writer

Authors use a text structure for a specific purpose. Cause-and-effect text structure tells what happened (cause) and the result (effect).

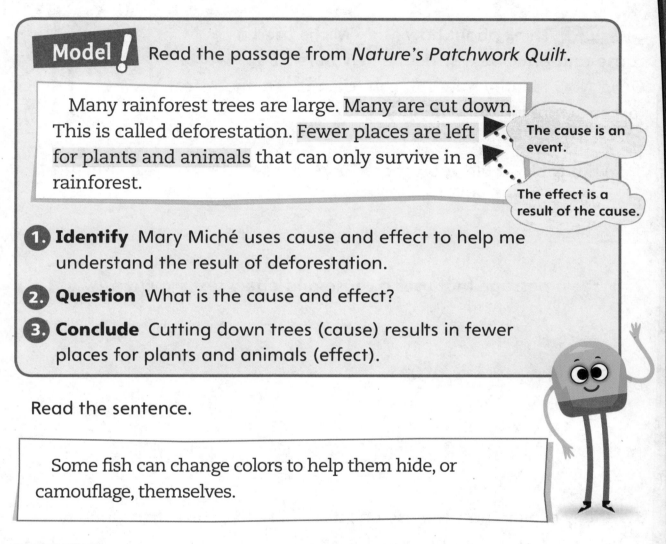

Model ! Read the passage from *Nature's Patchwork Quilt*.

Many rainforest trees are large. Many are cut down. This is called deforestation. Fewer places are left for plants and animals that can only survive in a rainforest.

The cause is an event.

The effect is a result of the cause.

1. Identify Mary Miché uses cause and effect to help me understand the result of deforestation.

2. Question What is the cause and effect?

3. Conclude Cutting down trees (cause) results in fewer places for plants and animals (effect).

Read the sentence.

Some fish can change colors to help them hide, or camouflage, themselves.

My TURN Follow the steps to analyze the passage. Describe the author's use of cause-and-effect text structure.

1. Identify Mary Miché uses cause and effect to help me understand

_____.

2. Question What is the cause and effect?

3. Conclude When fish _____ (the cause), this results in _____ (the effect).

Use text structures to organize information.

Write for a Reader

Writers use cause-and-effect text structure to explain what happened and the result of what happened.

My TURN Think about how Mary Miché used a cause-and-effect text structure in *Nature's Patchwork Quilt*. Now identify how you can use a cause-and-effect text structure in your writing.

1. What topic would you choose for a cause-and-effect text structure?

_____

_____

2. Write a passage that uses a cause-and-effect text structure.

_____

_____

_____

_____

_____

3. Briefly explain how the use of cause-and-effect text structure contributed to your purpose for writing.

_____

_____

_____

_____

Spell Contractions

Contractions combine two words by replacing at least one letter with an apostrophe ('). Contractions follow special spelling rules.

I + have = I've (delete *ha* and add apostrophe)
could + not = couldn't (delete *o* and add apostrophe)

My TURN Read the words. Sort them by the word that has been shortened. On another sheet of paper, write sentences using 3–5 contractions.

SPELLING WORDS		
I've	can't	didn't
won't	wouldn't	doesn't
let's	aren't	
couldn't	you've	

not	us	have
doesn't		**I've**
_____ _____	_____	_____
_____ _____		
_____		

High-Frequency Words

Study high-frequency words so you recognize them instantly. Write the following high-frequency words on the lines.

contain _____

front _____

Main Verbs and Helping Verbs

A **verb phrase** is made up of a **main verb** and one or more **helping verbs.** The main verb may describe action. The helping verb may help describe the time of the action. *Am, is,* and *are* show present time. *Was* and *were* show past time. To form the future tense, add *will* before a verb.

Verb Phrase	Helping Verb	Main Verb
I **am walking.**	am	walking
Birds **are chirping.**	are	chirping
The dog **is eating.**	is	eating
They **were riding** bikes.	were	riding
She **was walking.**	was	walking
He **will celebrate** the victory.	will	celebrate

My TURN Edit this draft by adding helping verbs that show the correct time of the action.

Yesterday, Tom walking his dog. When he got to the park, his friends playing basketball. He joined in.

Today, Tom is outside again. He riding his bike on the trail. His brothers riding with him. I walking to meet them now.

Edit for Legibility

Writers edit their handwriting to make sure it is **legible**, or easy to read. Use the checklist to help you write complete words, thoughts, and answers legibly in cursive.

IS MY CURSIVE WRITING LEGIBLE?

☐ Leave appropriate spaces between letters and words.

☐ Make sure each letter is formed and joined correctly.

☐ Check that each how-to step is numbered and lined up.

My TURN　Write legibly in cursive as you copy this how-to text.

This is how you grow a plant.

1. Fill a pot with good soil.
2. Place seeds in the pot.
3. Give the seeds proper light and water.

Be patient, and soon your plant will sprout!

Keep a slight slant in all letters.

My TURN　Use the checklist to edit one of your own drafts for legibility.

Edit for Complete Sentences with Subject-Verb Agreement

A **complete simple sentence** has a subject part and a predicate part. It expresses a complete thought. Edit using standard English conventions, including **subject-verb agreement**.

Singular Subject and Verb	Plural Subject and Verb
The wolf howls.	The wolves howl.
The habitat is protected.	The habitats are protected.

Sometimes there is more than one subject or one verb in a simple sentence.

- Rabbits and squirrels eat fruit.
- The bear eats and sleeps.
- The scientists observe and film the animals' behavior.

My TURN Edit each complete simple sentence for subject-verb agreement. Write the corrected sentence on the line.

1. Maisy watch the deer and take notes.

_____

2. Leo and Davin protects the animals from harmful plants.

_____

My TURN Edit one of your own drafts to check for complete simple sentences with subject-verb agreement.

Publish and Celebrate

Writers publish their how-to articles for many reasons, including

- Sharing their knowledge of a topic
- Helping a particular audience learn something new

My TURN Complete the sentences to describe your writing experience.

My favorite thing about writing a how-to article is _____

_____

_____

_____

The most important thing I learned about writing a how-to article is _____

_____

_____

_____

Someday I would like to write a how-to article about _____

_____

_____

_____

If my audience were younger students, I would change my how-to article by _____

_____

_____

_____

Prepare for Assessment

My TURN Follow a plan as you prepare to write a how-to article in response to a prompt.

1. **Make sure you understand the prompt.**
   You will receive an assignment called a writing prompt. Read the prompt carefully. <u>Underline</u> what kind of writing you will do. Highlight the topic you will be writing about.

   Prompt: Write a how-to article about helping an animal live in a certain habitat.

2. **Brainstorm.**
   List three animals and habitats you could write about. Highlight your favorite.

   _____

3. **Plan the steps of your how-to article.**
   Put the steps in order.

   Step 1: _____.

   Step 2: _____.

   Step 3: _____.

4. **Write a draft of your how-to article on a separate sheet of paper.**
   Start with an introduction that gives your article purpose and focus. End with a conclusion that ties everything together.

5. **After you finish, revise and edit your how-to article.**
   Reread your article to yourself.

Assessment

My TURN Before you write a how-to article for your assessment, rate how well you have learned the skills in this unit. Go back and review any skills you mark "No."

		Yes	No
Ideas and Organization	I can brainstorm and set a purpose.	☐	☐
	I can develop an engaging main idea.	☐	☐
	I can organize ideas into steps.	☐	☐
	I can organize steps into sequence.	☐	☐
	I can write an introduction and a conclusion.	☐	☐
Craft	I can write a headline and lead.	☐	☐
	I can add facts, details, and definitions.	☐	☐
	I can write a command.	☐	☐
	I can use linking words and phrases for coherence and clarity.	☐	☐
	I can include illustrations that add meaning.	☐	☐
	I can clarify steps using strong verbs.	☐	☐
Conventions	I can use prepositions and prepositional phrases.	☐	☐
	I can use adverbs and nouns.	☐	☐
	I can use coordinating conjunctions.	☐	☐
	I can edit for subject-verb agreement.	☐	☐

UNIT THEME
Interactions

TURN and TALK In a Word

With support from a partner, look back at each selection to choose and record a word that best shows the unit theme of *Interactions*. Then, use those words as you answer the Essential Question.

Wolf Island
by Celia Godkin

WEEK 3

Wolf Island

Theme word:

_____

BOOK CLUB

WEEK 2

Weird Friends
Unlikely Allies in the Animal Kingdom
by Jose Aruego and Ariane Dewey

Weird Friends

Theme word:

_____

BOOK CLUB

WEEK 1

Patterns in Nature
by Jennifer Rozines Roy and Gregory Roy

Patterns in Nature

Theme word:

_____

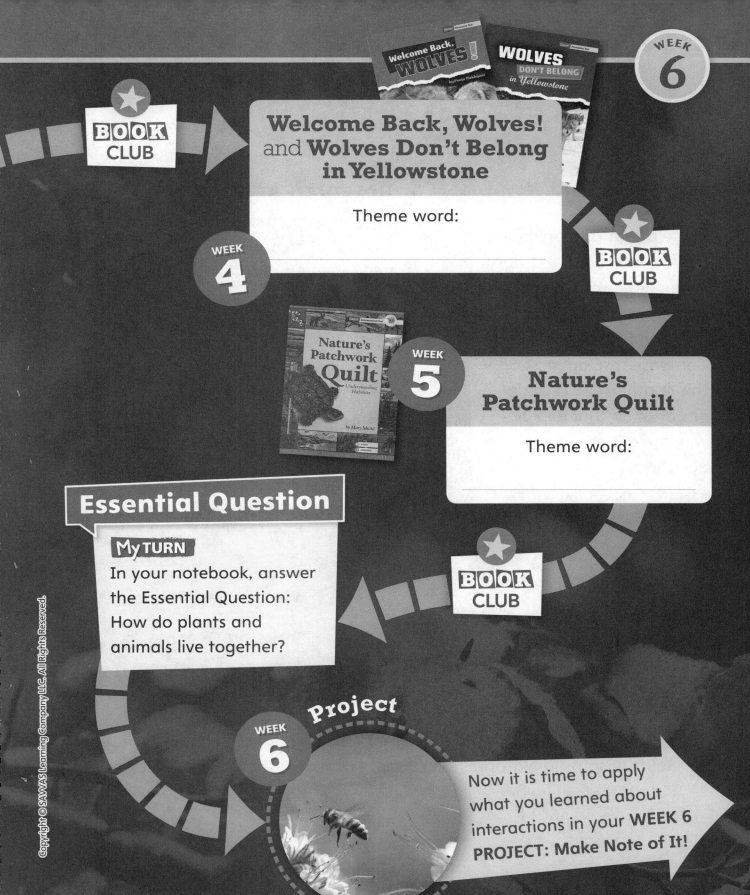

BOOK CLUB

Welcome Back, Wolves! and Wolves Don't Belong in Yellowstone

Theme word:

_____

WEEK 4

BOOK CLUB

WEEK 5

Nature's Patchwork Quilt

Theme word:

_____

Essential Question

My TURN

In your notebook, answer the Essential Question: How do plants and animals live together?

BOOK CLUB

WEEK 6 **Project**

Now it is time to apply what you learned about interactions in your **WEEK 6 PROJECT: Make Note of It!**

Make Note of IT!

Activity

Some plants and animals work together to help each other. Research a beneficial relationship between a plant and an animal. Compose a scrapbook on this relationship. Include information that explains why the relationship is beneficial to both.

RESEARCH

Research Articles

With your partner, read "Relationships in Nature" to generate questions you have about the topic for inquiry. Make a plan for researching information for your scrapbook.

1 **Relationships in Nature**

2 **Coral Reefs: Living Environments**

3 **Why We Need Plants**

Generate Questions

COLLABORATE Generate three questions you have about the information in "Relationships in Nature." Then, share your questions with the class.

1. _____

2. _____

3. _____

Use Academic Words

COLLABORATE In this unit, you learned many words related to the theme of *Interactions*. Work with your partner to add more academic vocabulary words to each category. Ask for help, if needed. If appropriate, use this vocabulary in your scrapbook.

Academic Vocabulary	Word Forms	Synonyms	Antonyms
prefer	preferable preferred preference	favor like care for	dislike refuse reject
features	featuring featured featureless	traits qualities characteristics	
investigate	investigated investigating investigation	examine explore research	ignore guess overlook
avoid	avoidance avoiding avoidable	miss escape stay away	seek meet welcome
associate	associates associated association	connect link relate	disassociate disconnect separate

Be Informed!

Details are words, phrases, and sentences that inform the reader about the topic.

Authors write **informational text** to inform or tell readers about a specific topic. When reading informational texts, look for

- a topic;
- photos and other text features, such as captions or tables, that support the topic;
- facts, definitions, and details that develop the topic; and
- a conclusion that sums up the information.

RESEARCH

COLLABORATE With your partner, read "Coral Reefs: Living Environments." Then, answer the questions about the text. Share the answers with your partner.

1. What is the topic? Identify a piece of evidence that supports the topic.

_____

_____

_____

2. What text feature best helped you understand the topic? Explain.

_____

_____

_____

3. Write two facts from the article.

_____

_____

_____

_____

Plan Your Research

COLLABORATE Before you begin researching plant and animal relationships, you will need to plan your research. Use the activity to choose and develop a topic.

Definition	Examples
DEFINE A TOPIC: Start out by thinking about plant/animal relationships. What do you know? What are you interested in finding out about various plant/animal relationships? Read the two sentences in the right column. Notice how a writer can narrow down the topic. Then, with your partner, complete the frames and decide on your topic.	I know a lot about <u>the rainforest.</u> I am interested in <u>the different trees that grow in the rainforest.</u> I know a lot about _____. I am interested in _____. My topic
DEVELOP THE TOPIC: Analyze your topic in order to inform your audience about it. You can do that by searching for information, such as • facts • definitions • details	**Fact:** The kapok tree can reach up to 200 feet in height. **Definition:** A *species* is a group of animals or plants that are similar. They can produce young or plants. **Details:** Palm trees grow hard fruits with soft centers. Many birds and animals such as toucans and monkeys eat the fruit.

With your partner, list some possible options for developing your topic.

DIGGING into a DATABASE

A **library database** is an online catalog that contains information from published works. You can search the database to evaluate whether a source is useful. Use text features, such as key words, sidebars, and hyperlinks, to locate information relevant to a given topic.

EXAMPLE Amelia wants to find out what kinds of rainforest plants can be used as medicine. Amelia does a search at the library by entering the key words *rainforest plants AND medicine* to narrow the search. Entering key words and the words *AND*, *NOT*, or *OR* is known as a Boolean search. This type of search can provide better results when a topic is specific.

---

rainforest plants AND medicine 🔍

Ana's Rainforest Walk by Marc Kim

A young scientist discovers natural remedies during her hike through a tropical rainforest.

Look inside.

The blue text at the top of each search result is the title of the book. Clicking on the hyperlink will send you to the location where the book can be found.

Rainforest: A Forest That Heals by Natalie Cohen

A complete list of rainforest plants and how they are used in modern medicine is provided.

Rainforest: A Forest That Heals

by Natalie Cohen

Look inside.

The cover art also serves as a hyperlink. Clicking on it will take you inside the pages of the book to give you an idea of what information you can find in it.

A summary of the book appears below the title.

COLLABORATE Use your library database and other books to gather information on a plant and animal relationship. You will use this information to create a scrapbook. With your partner, discuss your findings and choose a relationship that helps both the plant and animal.

Name of book/author:

Where found:

Notes:

Name of book/author:

Where found:

Notes:

Discuss your search results. Do you need to change your key words to find more specific information?

Inform Me!

Informational writing informs readers about a topic. It organizes information logically and includes elements such as text features. An informational scrapbook presents facts, details, and images in visually interesting ways.

Before you begin writing, decide how to organize your scrapbook. Will you

- organize facts in any particular order, such as order of importance?
- provide definitions or examples?
- include text features, such as illustrations, sections, or bold text?

> **COLLABORATE** Read the Student Model. Work with your partner to recognize the characteristics and structures of informational writing.

Now You Try It!

Discuss the checklist with a partner. Work together to follow the steps as you create your scrapbook page.

Make sure your scrapbook

- ☐ introduces your topic.
- ☐ organizes related information about the topic.
- ☐ develops the topic with facts, definitions, and details.
- ☐ uses text features such as illustrations, captions, sections, tables, and bold text.

Student Model

Rainforest Trees

Underline the topic.

Strangler
Fig Tree

Walking
Palm Tree

Peach Palm
Tree

Put a star next to the text feature.

Tree Type	Fun Facts
strangler fig	Bats and birds use the trunk of the strangler fig for their homes.
peach palm	Oil from the nuts of the peach palm is used for cooking.
walking palm	This tree is known as the walking palm because it can move through a forest as it grows new roots.

Highlight a detail about a tree.

Citing Sources!

A **works cited page** is a list of all the sources that were used in a research report or other project. It appears at the end of the report or project. The chart shows how to cite three types of sources.

Type of Source	Information to Include	Example
Book	Author, last name first. (If there is more than one author, list them in the order in which they appear on the title page.) *Title of Book*. Publisher, year of publication.	Rice, William B. *Amazon Rainforest*. Teacher Created Materials, 2012.
Article in a reference book	Author. "Title of Article." *Title of Reference Book*. Year published. Print or online.	Bigg, Michael A. "Whale." *The World Book Encyclopedia*. 1992. Print.
Online source	Author, if known. "Title of Web Page." Title of Web Site, date of site. URL. Date of your visit to URL or when you accessed it.	Schiffman, Richard. "Crazy Companions." Company X, 2017. http://www.companyx.com/about/facts.html. Accessed June 1, 2017.

RESEARCH

COLLABORATE Read "Why We Need Plants." Then, with your partner, think of a source that includes additional facts about the topic. Show how you would cite the source on a works cited page.

Author's Name	
Title of Article	
Title of Complete Work (if known)	
Date of Publication	

COLLABORATE Read the paragraph from a research source and answer the questions. Then, gather your sources and create a works cited page for your scrapbook.

Rainforests to the Rescue

by Robin Landis, PhD

from *Our Green Times*

The rainforests of the world make up less than 10 percent of Earth's surface. However, almost half of all plant species live in the rainforests. Some of the medicines that we need and use come from rainforests. Many of the ingredients used in modern medicine come from rainforest plants. Medicines are only one of the many resources our rainforests have to offer.

1. Who wrote this article?

_____

2. What is the name of the magazine that the article is from?

_____

3. What are three sets of key words you might use to do an online search for this article?

_____

_____

Include Visuals/MEDIA

Writers can make their writing stronger by including **visuals** and different **media**, or formats for sharing information.

Visuals make your writing stand out. A visual can be a photo, illustration, diagram, graph, or table that is used to make a piece of writing easier to understand. Photographs and illustrations help your readers visualize your topic more clearly.

A **diagram** points out special features in a picture. The labels help your readers better understand your topic.

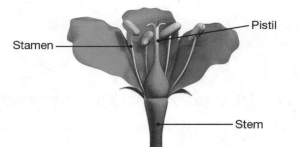

Graphs and **tables** give your readers additional information using pictures, numbers, and lists. There are many different types.

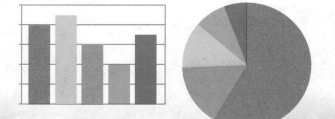
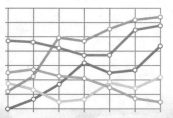

COLLABORATE With your partner, brainstorm which forms of visuals and media will make your scrapbook more interesting and help it to stand out. Then, go online to find some examples. Finally, work together to design a cover for your scrapbook.

Type of media:

Source:

How would it make the scrapbook more interesting?

Type of visual:

Source:

How would it help a reader to better understand the text?

Revise

Clarity Reread your scrapbook page with your partner. Have you included

☐ details that support the topic?

☐ text that is easy to understand?

☐ definitions and examples?

Revise for Clarity

The writers of the scrapbook page began with a first draft. They read their draft and noticed that some information was not very clear. They revised some sentences by adding details to make ideas clearer and more interesting.

Bats and birds use   their
The trunk of the strangler fig is used for homes.

Oil from the nuts of
The peach palm is used for cooking.

Edit

Conventions Read your scrapbook pages again. Have you

- ☐ checked the spelling of all words?
- ☐ used the correct punctuation in your sentences, including apostrophes and commas?
- ☐ capitalized all proper names and places?
- ☐ made sure all subjects and verbs agree?

Peer Review

COLLABORATE Exchange your scrapbook with another group. As you read, try to recognize characteristics of informational writing, such as how the topic is introduced and how the information is organized. Then, discuss ways in which the author could use visuals or text features to make the writing easier to understand.

Time to Celebrate!

COLLABORATE When you finish a research project, it is important and fun to share your work. To communicate your ideas clearly and politely,

- make eye contact by looking at your audience.
- speak at a speed that is easy to understand.
- speak at a volume that is appropriate for a small, indoor group.
- enunciate, or pronounce words correctly.
- thank your audience for listening.

Follow these rules to share your scrapbook with another group. Be sure to read the text and show all the visual elements.

Reflect on Your Project

My TURN Think about your scrapbook. How was the information organized? How did text features support your writing? What could you change to improve your scrapbook? Write your thoughts here.

Organization and Text Features

_____

_____

Ideas for Improvement

_____

_____

Reflect on Your Goals

Look back at your unit goals.
Use a different color to rate yourself again.

Reflect on Your Reading

What did you learn from the texts that you read independently during this unit?

_____

_____

_____

_____

_____

Reflect on Your Writing

What did you like most about the writing you created in this unit?

_____

_____

_____

_____

_____

How to Use a Glossary

This glossary can help you understand the meaning, pronunciation, and syllabication of some of the words in this book. The entries in this glossary are in alphabetical order. The guide words at the top of each page show the first and last words on the page. If you cannot find a word, check a print or online dictionary. You would use a dictionary just as you would a glossary. To use a digital resource, type the word you are looking for in the search box at the top of the page.

Example glossary entry:

The entry word is in bold type. It shows how the word is spelled and divided into syllables.

The pronunciation is in parentheses. It also shows which syllables are stressed.

ad·ap·ta·tions (ad′ ap tā′ shənz), *NOUN*. changes in plants and animals that help them survive

The definition shows what the word means.

Part-of-speech label shows the function of an entry word.

My TURN

Find and write the meaning of the word *crouching*. Say the word aloud.

_____

Write the syllabication of the word. _____
Write the part of speech of the word. _____
How did the part of speech help you understand how the word is used?

_____
_____

TURN and TALK Discuss how you can find the meaning of a word that is not in this glossary.

Aa

ad•ap•ta•tions
(ad′ ap tā′ shənz), *NOUN*. changes in plants and animals that help them survive

a•maz•ing (ə mā′ zing), *ADJECTIVE*. causing great wonder or surprise

as•so•ci•ate (ə sō′ shē āt), *VERB*. to make a connection between two people or things

a•vail•a•ble (ə vā′ lə bəl), *ADJECTIVE*. ready to use

a•void (ə void′), *VERB*. to stay away from a person, place, or thing

Bb

bal•ance (bal′ əns), *NOUN*. enough different plants and animals to keep a habitat healthy

bar•ing (bâr′ ing), *VERB*. showing

bi•o•di•ver•si•ty
(bī′ ō di vûr′ si tē), *NOUN*. the existence of many different kinds of plants and animals in an environment

Pronunciation Guide

Use the pronunciation guide to help you pronounce the words correctly.

a in *hat*	ō in *open*	sh in *she*
ā in *age*	ȯ in *all*	th in *thin*
â in *care*	ô in *order*	ŦH in *then*
ä in *far*	oi in *oil*	zh in *measure*
e in *let*	ou in *out*	ə = a in *about*
ē in *equal*	u in *cup*	ə = e in *taken*
ėr in *term*	u̇ in *put*	ə = i in *pencil*
i in *it*	ü in *rule*	ə = o in *lemon*
ī in *ice*	ch in *child*	ə = u in *circus*
o in *hot*	ng in *long*	

bored • globe

bored (bôrd), *ADJECTIVE*. not interested in something

brood•ed (brüd′ id), *VERB*. worried or fretted

Cc

cam•ou•flage (kam′ ə fläzh), *VERB*. hide or make harder to see one's natural surroundings

com•pe•ti•tion (kom′ pə tish′ ən), *NOUN*. the act of trying to win something

crouch•ing (krouch′ ing), *VERB*. bending down

cus•tom (kus′ təm), *NOUN*. something that people have done for a long time

Dd

de•pend•ed (di pend′ id), *VERB*. counted or relied on

dis•cov•er•y (dis kuv′ ər ē), *NOUN*. something found for the first time

dreams (drēmz), *VERB*. has a detailed goal or purpose

Ee

e•lim•i•nat•ed (i lim′ ə nāt id), *VERB*. removed

e•merg•es (i mėrj′ ez), *VERB*. to come out of a hidden place

ex•po•sure (ek spō′ zhər), *NOUN*. the condition of being unprotected from severe weather

Ff

fea•tures (fē′ chərz), *NOUN*. the details or specific traits of something

fierce (firs), *ADJECTIVE*. wild or dangerous

flex•ing (fleks′ ing), *VERB*. curling

food chain (füd′ chān), *NOUN*. a series of living things that depend on each other as food sources

foot•path (fu̇t′ path), *NOUN*. a narrow walking path for people

Gg

globe (glōb), *NOUN*. an object shaped like a ball

Hh

hab•i•tat (hab′ ə tat), *NOUN*. the natural home of a plant or animal

Ii

im•mune (i myün′), *ADJECTIVE*. not affected by something, such as an illness

in•ter•de•pend•ence (in′ tər di pen′ dens), *NOUN*. when things depend or rely on one another

in•ves•ti•gate (in ves′ tə gāt), *VERB*. to examine or look closely at something

Ll

lack (lak), *NOUN*. the state of not having something

land•scape (land′ skāp), *NOUN*. the natural features seen in a particular area

Mm

mag•nif•i•cent (mag nif′ ə sent), *ADJECTIVE*. very wonderful or beautiful

moun•tain•side (moun′ tən sīd), *NOUN*. the sloping side of a mountain

mul•ti•plied (mul′ tə plīd′), *VERB*. increased greatly in number

mur•mur•ing (mėr′ mər ing), *NOUN*. a soft, continuous sound

Nn

na•ture (nā′ chər), *NOUN*. the things around us not made by humans

no•mad•ic (nō mad′ ik), *ADJECTIVE*. moving around a lot

Oo

oc•ca•sion (ə kā′ zhən), *NOUN*. a special time or event

or•gan•i•za•tion (ôr′ gə nə zā′ shən), *NOUN*. the process of putting things in order

Pp

pat•terns (pat′ ərns), *NOUN*. sets of things that repeat in order

pop•u•la•tion (pop′ yə lā′ shən), *NOUN*. the number of animals or people living in a place

GLOSSARY

pouch (pouch), *NOUN.* a small bag that closes with a piece of string

pred•a•tors (pred/ ə tərz), *NOUN.* animals that live by eating other animals

pre•fer (pri fėr/), *VERB.* to like one thing more than another thing

prep•a•ra•tions (prep/ ə rā/ shənz), *NOUN.* activities to get ready for something

pro•tec•tion (prə tek/ shən), *NOUN.* safety

proud (proud), *ADJECTIVE.* feeling good about oneself or something

Rr

re•in•tro•duced (ri in/ trə düst/), *VERB.* brought an animal or plant back into an area

re•joic•ing (ri jois/ ing), *NOUN.* actions and feelings of great happiness

re•peat (ri pēt/), *VERB.* to happen over and over

Ss

sat•is•fied (sat/ i sfīd), *ADJECTIVE.* happy or pleased

se•quence (sē/ kwəns), *NOUN.* a series of things in order

shield (shēld), *VERB.* to protect by covering

sol•i•tar•y (sol/ ə ter/ ē), *ADJECTIVE.* single or living alone

solve (solv), *VERB.* to find the answer to a problem

spe•cies (spē/ shēz), *NOUN.* a group of living things that are the same in most ways

swipe (swīp), *VERB.* to hit

sym•me•try (sim/ ə trē), *NOUN.* being the same on both sides

Ww

well-be•ing (wel/ bē/ ing), *NOUN.* health and comfort

CREDITS

Text

Arte Publico Press

The Golden Flower by Nina Jaffe Is reprinted with permission from the publisher (©2005 Arte Publico Press - University of Houston).

Dawn Publications

Nature's Patchwork Quilt, authored by Mary Miché and illustrated by Consie Powell. Reprinted by permission from Dawn Publications.

Fitzhenry & Whiteside Limited
Wolf Island by Celia Godkin, Fitzhenry & Whiteside Limited. Reprinted by permission.

Henry Holt & Company

Grandma and the Great Gourd by Chitra Banerjee Divakaruni, reprinted by Henry Holt Books for Young Readers. Caution: Users are warned that this work is protected under copyright laws and downloading is strictly prohibited. The right to reproduce or transfer the work via any medium must be secured with Macmillan Publishing Group, LLC d/b/a Henry Holt & Company.

Houghton Mifflin Harcourt Publishing Company

Weird Friends: Unlikely Friends in the Animal Kingdom by Jose Aruego and Ariane Dewey. Copyright© 2002 by Jose Aruego and Ariane Dewey. Reprinted by permission of Houghton Mifflin Harcourt Publishing Company. All rights reserved.

The Rosen Publishing Group Inc.

Living in Deserts by Tea Benduhn. Reprinted by permission from Gareth Stevens Publishing. Patterns in Nature by Jennifer Rozines Roy and Gregory Roy. Reprinted by permission from Cavendish Square Publishing.

Photographs

Photo locators denoted as follows: Top (T), Center (C), Bottom (B), Left (L), Right (R), Background (Bkgd)

8 (BL) George Burba/Shutterstock, (Bkgd) Mangm Srisukh Stock Photo/Shutterstock; **9** Bobby Model/National Geographic/Getty Images **14** (T) Dmitry Rukhlenko/Shutterstock, (C) Neo Studio/Shutterstock, (B) Daniel J. Rao/Shutterstock; **15** (T) Zoltan Szabo Photography/Shutterstock, (B) Amlan Mathur/Shutterstock; **62** Mary-Joan Gerson; **98** NotionPic/Shutterstock; **130** (T) Robert Burch/Alamy Stock Photo, (B) Nathapol Kongseang/Shutterstock; (Bkgd) Roserunn/Shutterstock,(BL) Vvoe/Shutterstock; **134** Used with permission from Gareth Stevens Publishing.; **135** Bobby Model/National Geographic/Getty Images; **137** (B) Tim Bewer/Lonely Planet Images/Getty Images; **139** (T) Maria Stenzel/National Geographic/Getty Images; **141** (B) Dean Conger/Corbis Historical/Getty Images; **142** (T) Torsten Blackwood/AFP/Getty Images; **143** (B) Jose Fuste Raga/Corbis Documentary/Getty Images; **145** (B) Frans Sellies/Moment Open/Getty Images; **146** (T) Christian Goupi/Age Fotostock/Alamy Stock Photo; **147** (B) Kazuyoshi Nomachi/Corbis Documentary/Getty Images; **148** Dmitry Pichugin /Shutterstock; **149** (B) Elena Petrova/Alamy Stock Photo; **152** (B) Charles Bowman/Robertharding/Alamy Stock Photo; **153** (T) Frederic J. Brown/AFP/Getty Images; **174** Lik Studio/Shutterstock; **175** (T) Maria Uspenskaya/Shutterstock, (B) Onebluelight/E+/Getty Images; **178** Photo of Nina Jaffe Is reprinted with permission from the publisher(© 2000 Arte Publico Press - University of Houston); **211** Pla2na/Shutterstock; **212** Pla2na/Shutterstock; **216** Sigur/Shutterstock; **218** Community Garden/Alamy Stock Photo; **220** Ubonwan Poonpracha/Shutterstock; **225** Hero Images/Getty Images; **228** (BL)123RF, (Bkgd) Ondrej Prosicky/Shutterstock; **229** Nagel Photography/Shutterstock **234** (Bkgd) Julian W/Shutterstock; **235** FotoRequest/Shutterstock; **234** (T) Simon Eeman/Shutterstock, (B) Chesapeake Images/Shutterstock; **238** Used with permission from Jennifer Rozines Roy.; **239** Mick Roessler/Corbis/Getty Images; **240** (BC) Danlogan/iStock/Getty Images; **241** (T) Ron Watts/Corbis/Getty Images; **242** (L) Veniamin Kraskov/Shutterstock; **243** (CL) Brand X Pictures/Stockbyte/Getty Images, (BL) Amphaiwan/Shutterstock; **244** (BR) Paul Pellegrino/Shutterstock; **244** (TR) Prostock-studio/Shutterstock; **245** (CL) Craig Tuttle/Corbis Documentary/Getty Images; **246** Irin-k/Shutterstock; **247** (T) Power,Syred/Science Source, (TL) Power and Syred/Science Source, (BL) Craig Tuttle/Corbis Documentary/Getty Images; **248** (T) Sabina Pittak/Shutterstock, (B) Giuliano Coman/Shutterstock; **249** (B) Robert Glusic/Corbis/Getty Images; **250** (C) Pavel Ganchev - Paf/Shutterstock, (CL) George D. Lepp/Corbis Documentary/Getty Images, (CR) Dave and Les Jacobs/Blend Images/Getty Images, (BC) Olga Gavrilova/Shutterstock; **251** (TL) Sari Oneal/Shutterstock; **252** (TC) Anest/Shutterstock, (BC) Watperm/Shutterstock; **253** (B) Tom & Dee Ann McCarthy/Corbis/Getty Images; **270** (T) Olegbush/Shutterstock, (B) Victor Lapaev/Shutterstock, (C) 7th Son Studio/Shutterstock, (Bkgd) Andrzej Kubik/Shutterstock; **271** (T) Pavel Krasensky/Shutterstock, (B) EcoPrint/Shutterstock; **306** (T) AlinaMD/Shutterstock, (B) Standret/Shutterstock; **306** VideoProkopchuk/Shutterstock; **307** (T) Ondrej Chvatal/Shutterstock, (B) Marcin Jucha/Shutterstock; **310** Celia Godkin, 2017.; **340** (T) Vesna Kriznar/Shutterstock, (B) Hartl/Blickwinkel/Alamy Stock Photo; **341** (T) PhotocechCZ/Shutterstock, (B) Alexey Stiop/123RF; **345** Nagel Photography/Shutterstock; **346** Michelle Holihan/Shutterstock; **348** Nature and Science/Alamy Stock Photo; **349** Pngstudio/123RF; **350** Reinhard Hölzl/Imagebroker/Alamy Stock Photo; **351** Andreanita/123RF; **354** (L) William Campbell/Corbis Historical/Getty Images,(R) Gina Kelly/Alamy Stock Photo; **353** Wildlife GmbH/Alamy Stock Photo; **355** RiverNorthPhotography/iStock/Getty Images; **356** Neale Haynes/Buzz Pictures/Alamy

Stock Photo; **357** Maciej Bledowski/Shutterstock; **358** Thomas Kokta/Photographer's Choice RF/ Getty Images; **359** Vasily Smirnov/iStock/Getty Images; **376** (TC) LiskaM/Shutterstock; (CL) Olgysha/ Shutterstock; (BC),(BR) Rattiya Thongdumhyu/ Shutterstock,(T) Kanokwan14002/Shutterstock, (C) Robuart/Shutterstock, (Bkgd) KittyVector/ Shutterstock; **377** (T) Africa Studio/Shutterstock, (C) NaturesMomentsuk/Shutterstock, (B) Picturepartners/ Shutterstock; **380** Used with permission from Dawn Publications.; **414** Andy.M/Shutterstock; **418** GagliardiImages/Shutterstock; **420** AustralianCamera/ Shutterstock; **422** Guentermanaus/Shutterstock; **424** (TL) Pulsar Imagens/Alamy Stock Photo, (TC) PiXXart/Shutterstock, (TR) Naris Visitsin /123RF; (B) Sciencepics/Shutterstock; **427** Steve Byland/ Shutterstock.

Illustrations

17 Valeria Cis; **58–59** André Jolicoeur; **61, 133, 237, 343** Olga & Aleksey Ivanov; **97, 379** Valentina Belloni; **99–113** Maine Diaz; **177, 309** Ilana Exelby; **216, 222–223, 346, 421, 424** Rob Schuster; **273** Ken Bowser; **418** Karen Minot